Super Secrets
of
Successful Executive
Job Search

**EVERYTHING YOU NEED TO KNOW TO FIND
AND SECURE THE EXECUTIVE POSITION YOU
DESERVE**

SIMON GRAY

Super Secrets
of
Successful Executive Job Search

Published by Career Codex
Website: https://careercodex.com
First published in Great Britain in 2015

Book cover © 2015 Simon Gray and
designed by Sainah Benz M. Alonzo
Photographs taken by Sammy Smiles Photography

This book was written in the United Kingdom using British English. As a result, readers from other countries may find minor spelling and grammatical differences.

A catalogue record for this book can be obtained from the British Library.

Set in Times New Roman
Copyright © 2015 Simon Gray
ISBN-13: 978-0-9931783-1-3
ISBN-10: 0993178316

Praise for

Simon Gray
and
Super Secrets of Successful Executive Job Search

'This guide left me completely clear that I am the master of my fate. Simon shares not only the tips and skills I need to secure my next role but also ruthlessly anticipates the 'yes but... my situation is different' arguments, completely disarming those inner voices. A very empowering read, applicable in other areas of my life where lack of confidence and skilled procrastination get in the way.'
— **Carole Harvey – CFO and Non-Executive Director**

'In this book you'll find both inspiration and practical solutions to the maze that is the executive job market. I wish I'd had access to this book years ago when I was looking for my ideal position. I love the simplicity and common sense, the insights and the pragmatic style captured throughout. If you're looking for the right executive position for you, then this book is a must read.'
— **Lisa Spencer-Arnell – Author and Leadership**
  Development Coach

'This book is a great read! It is packed full of practical ideas that are simple to understand and implement. It's very easy to follow and gets to the point quickly. The chapters give clear direction and are easy to digest – you can put things into practice immediately. Simon's style of writing really draws you into his story and experience!'
— **Adrian Peck – Professional Speaker Trainer and**
  Master Practitioner of NLP

DEDICATION

To my fantastic wife, Sammy, and my two boys,
Charlie and Maxi – I love you all
xxx xxx xxx

CONTENTS

TWO QUOTES AND A THOUGHT

'Observe the masses and do the opposite.'
— **Walt Disney**

'If you can keep your head when all about you are losing theirs…!'
— **Rudyard Kipling**

'If success in the executive job market is about standing out, how can doing what everyone else is doing ever lead to success?'
— **Simon Gray**

A WORD OF WARNING

This is a journey that will change your life for the better – are you ready?

If you're reading this – congratulations! You've uncovered the book that can help you stand out in the executive job market to find and then secure the executive position you want.

If you're in the executive job market and want to take charge of your career, you need this book.

This book is for you if you're currently in a senior executive position and wanting to advance your career, or currently in a management role and aspiring to the next level.

It's for you whether you're currently in the executive job market at the very start of your search or have been in the game for a while now but have yet to find success.

Forget waiting for the right opportunity to be advertised, by then it's often too late. It's time to grab the executive job market by the scruff of the neck – it's time for you to take control of your own destiny!

This book will give you a new way of thinking and a completely different approach to what your competition is doing in the executive job market. It will make you stand out from the crowd and enable you to open doors you never knew existed or previously found closed.

By absorbing everything in this book and taking the recommended action, whatever you want from your future career is firmly within your grasp.

However, be warned – your existing beliefs will be challenged and your comfort zone tested. Without a little discomfort, growth is impossible - embrace this discomfort and trust in the fact that it will lead you to a better and more fulfilling future.

Make copious notes and review them regularly – highlight what resonates with you and especially what challenges you.

ACKNOWLEDGMENTS

A big thank-you to Rick, who helped me at the start of this journey – our conversations helped shape this book more than you know.

To Melissa G. Lewis for her dedication, patience and attention to detail – I hope this is the first of many projects we'll work on together.

INTRODUCTION

COFFEE WITH CLIVE

It's early May, and I'm in Costa Coffee waiting for Clive. Sipping on my Americano, I glance to the top of the stairs to try to identify him from his LinkedIn profile and consider what my first impressions will be following our phone conversation earlier in the month.

The noise of the coffee shop provides an unwanted distraction with families and friends engaging in chit-chat, which contrasts with what Clive and I are there to talk about.

He arrives, and I recognise him instantly from his profile picture – a good start.

Clive has flown in from Switzerland to meet me. He's a senior executive who's reached the pinnacle of his career as vice president and managing director of a large international manufacturing business. He's well presented, confident, articulate and everything you'd expect of someone of his stature and experience.

However, he has one problem.

Through no fault of his own, he's been in the executive job market for a year and a half. Despite being highly experienced with a solid track record of progression and achievement, he's had very few interviews.

To use his own words: 'I just don't understand why my CV isn't working for me!'

Clive's frustration was one I'd heard many times in the past. He was following what everyone else in the job market was doing as if a blueprint for success and as a result, was failing to secure the opportunity he so desired.

The longer this had gone on, the more frustrated and despondent he had become, meaning that even if the perfect opportunity had fallen at his doorstep, he would have been in no position to capitalise on it.

But why would someone so capable and experienced, with a great personality, find himself on the executive job market for so long?

As an executive in a senior position, you are surrounded by people. You may have a large team to delegate responsibility to and will no doubt have other senior colleagues for counsel and advice. Hopefully, you're well remunerated and able to provide a comfortable living for yourself and your family. You represent the organisation you work for at the highest level and are the consummate professional who doesn't take things personally.

When you find yourself on the executive job market, the game changes. Suddenly your support system is gone, your salary and benefits are gone, and furthermore, you start to take things personally. Things are no longer happening to the organisation you work for; they're happening to you – or in Clive's case, the problem was that not much was happening at all.

Whether you find yourself on the executive job market unintentionally or through a conscious decision sparked by the desire for change or advancement, if things don't happen quickly enough in line with your expectations, the job market at some point is likely to take its toll.

Clive didn't understand the executive job market – it was an alien environment to him and one in which he had little experience.

The lack of activity had started to negatively impact him, and by his own admission, he had started to lose confidence. He described his current position to me as being in a 'terrible wilderness', not knowing where to turn or what to do.

He had no plan in place – with no clear focus, he was simply reacting to what the executive job market threw at him, which wasn't very much. Instead of dining at the table as a king, he was reliant on the scraps from the table.

Finally, he lacked the skills to win in battle – the finer details of how to conduct the day-to-day tasks involved in positioning himself ahead of his competition to stand out.

Clive was not the first client I had ever worked with, but his transformation was one of the greatest.

As we worked together, he became clear on the position he wanted and how to go about getting it. He moved from reactive to proactive, and as I observed his newfound understanding of how the executive job market really works and his position in it, it was extremely rewarding to see his energy levels rise and his confidence grow.

By November, he had secured the position he desired with a growing and expanding organisation. He was back to his former self and extremely excited for the future.

This book will educate and inspire you to believe different things about the executive job market and your position in it, to use a different thought process than your competition uses, and to take focused and deliberate action to find the executive position you want, on your terms.

This is not a boring textbook full of theoretical advice. Instead, it is full of anecdotes and practical advice that works based on real-life experience.

I look forward to taking you on this journey, but before I do, I will leave you with a final word from Clive:

'Simon has developed a most effective process for anyone wanting to consider a change of position or career. His process brings great structure and discipline to the job hunt to exponentially widen and enhance your prospects for the next career move.

'He literally transforms your view of the entire process, and I would highly recommend Simon to anyone – whether currently working or in between jobs – who wants to take that next step in his or her career.'

BURNING BOATS

I've always been someone who practices what I preach, and I've never been afraid to burn my boats.

Legend has it that the Vikings, having landed on new shores to conquer, would burn their boats. With no opportunity for retreat, they were left with two options – death or victory!

Talk about something to focus the mind and to fuel determination.

Now, I'm no Viking, but I have been brave and focused enough to shape my own career and pursue my passions.

Having graduated from university, I trained as a chartered accountant with KPMG. Auditing not being my first love, on qualification I approached a recruitment agency to help find me a job in industry.

To cut a long story short, I changed direction and ended up

working for them as a recruitment consultant.

After a two-year career break in Japan, I came back to the UK and started my own recruitment business two weeks before the financial crisis hit in 2008.

Talk about burning boats…!

In a recession, the first thing employers do is hang a notice outside their door that says 'recruitment freeze', and candidates tend to batten down the hatches and believe that their current job is the safest place to be. It tends to kill the whole market when your clients and candidates are not in the game.

My time in Japan had prepared me well. I'd gone over to Tokyo for a life experience and because it scared me. As a keen martial artist, I'd read a book called *Angry White Pyjamas* by Robert Twigger – the true story of a guy who enrolled in one of the toughest martial arts courses in the world, the Yoshinkan Aikido Senshusei Programme.

Senshusei is 11 months of blood, sweat and tears training with the Tokyo Riot Police in the art of aikido, and it was to be one of the most profound and influential experiences of my life.

Inspired by the book, I'd packed my bag and travelled to Japan to experience it for myself – there went another boat!

Aikido teaches you to move forward proactively at all times to engage your opponent – there is no retreat. More importantly, and unlike other martial arts, it teaches you to use your attackers' energy against them; you never fight force with force.

What I learnt helped me build a successful business in a recession and also underpins many of the principles in this book. Discipline and determination are essential traits for a martial artist and are also fundamental to finding success in the executive job market.

I still had one boat left to burn, though; despite running a profitable recruitment company that was experiencing rapid growth coming out of a recession, I decided to leave!

People questioned my sanity, but recruitment was no longer my passion. Using my knowledge and experience to empower jobseekers at all levels to find their own way and success in the job market was.

In my business, I'd spent considerable time interviewing and advising executive candidates on how best to approach the job market. Because I was running a recruitment company and was in the business of making money from placing people in jobs, my advice probably should have been the following:

Stick with us and we'll find you a position. Things are picking up, and it hopefully won't take too long.

In my heart, though, I knew that as much as I would have liked to place everyone I ever interviewed in a job, it would never happen. It's not the way the executive job market works, as you'll find out through reading this book.

Not wanting to give false hope to candidates who had come to me in good faith for help, I changed the structure of my interviews. I moved away from a detailed analysis and trawl through their CV toward giving advice on how to approach the executive job market in the right way.

With only 45 minutes to an hour for our meeting, there was very little time to communicate what I needed to get across. Driven by this and the fact that I was getting sick of the sound of my own voice (repeating myself over and over), I decided to write a book.

Super Secrets of the Successful Jobseeker, published by Harriman House, has been hugely successful and has helped many people find their own success in the job market.

This book builds on some of the concepts in my first book but is written specifically with senior executives in mind. It is the culmination of my observations and experiences sitting between employers and candidates in the recruitment industry for over ten years.

Career Codex is the business I created to deliver this knowledge far and wide. I'm extremely proud to have helped people from all over the world achieve their dream of finding and then securing the executive position they deserve.

If you've already read *Super Secrets of the Successful Jobseeker*, please read on; this book takes things to a whole new level and provides education, strategies and tactics that I'm sharing publicly for the very first time.

I'd love to hear your stories of success from reading this book and wish you every success in the future.

Simon Gray

To contact me, please visit: https://careercodex.com or e-mail: simon.gray@careercodex.com

HOW TO GET
THE MOST FROM THIS BOOK

This book is best read from start to finish.

Many senior executives I work with in the job market want my opinion and critique of their CV at the outset. Yet as you read on, you'll discover that your CV, also known as your résumé, is one of the least important elements in finding success in the executive job market.

Strong foundations are essential and can never be overlooked. A house without firm foundations will crumble over time, and as time is often the enemy of those in the job market, gaining a solid understanding of the executive job market and your own psychology is the only place to start.

If you have a pressing interview or are at the offer and negotiation stage, please feel free to jump ahead to the relevant chapters. However, to gain the most from this book, please come back at some point and read it from the beginning.

This book is broken up into four key areas:

Environment – how the executive job market really works and how to therefore position yourself successfully to stand out.

Psychology – how what you believe ultimately leads to your success or failure in the executive job market.

Planning – how to clearly define and communicate the executive job you want.

Process – the more traditional tools to finding job market success but approached from a completely different standpoint (e.g. CV and cover letter composition, interview technique, social media and professional networking).

Think of **environment** and **psychology** as the foundations of your house, **planning** as the detailed architectural drawings, and **process** as the bricks and mortar you'll use to construct the property of your dreams.

Using the framework and methodology in this book, you'll be empowered to:

1. Uncover a higher number of executive opportunities in a shorter period of time.

2. Generate a higher probability of converting executive opportunities into offers.

3. Negotiate a more competitive starting salary and benefits package.

4. Manage your own career and job search both now and in the future.

Get ready – this book also contains some hidden surprises!

Rick, a senior executive in the power, industrial and aerospace sector – one of my very first clients – said that after following the steps outlined in this book, he found the process one that not only made him more effective in the executive job market but also made him a better person in life.

THE EXECUTIVE
JOB MARKET ENVIRONMENT

Unless you as a senior executive understand the make-up and complexities of the environment you operate in, it can be an uphill struggle to attack the executive job market in the correct way to find the success you deserve.

Knowledge is power, as they say, and knowledge starts with understanding the lie of the land.

This chapter will give you a detailed understanding of why the executive job market exists, the key players in it and, most importantly, what motivates the players into action.

Why the executive job market exists

The executive job market exists to serve the needs of two groups of people:

1. Businesses or organisations that have a need to hire for a variety of reasons, including replacing someone who has left, setting up a new division or gaining access to new markets.

2. Executive jobseekers that are looking for their next move as a result of relocation, redundancy, career advancement or the need for change.

Although a business is an entity in its own right, it is the people within the organisation who drive any recruitment process, and executive jobseekers are individual people looking to find an opportunity in the executive job market.

These people have one thing in common – the process is often *painful* and *misunderstood* for both!

Employers find the recruitment process a distraction from running their business and, aside from larger organisations with dedicated resourcing teams, often have limited experience in how to hire successfully.

Executive jobseekers often face the pressure of not earning a salary (particularly as a result of redundancy) or having to find time to do their search outside of normal working hours.

Both parties have to dedicate *time* to the process, which often adds to the *pain*.

When we as consumers purchase a new computer or a washing machine, we're buying a standardised product that comes off a production line. It's been rigorously tested and usually comes with a guarantee in case something goes wrong.

Conversely, people are completely unique; there is no such thing as a standardised person, and people rarely come with a money-back guarantee!

Think of people you have hired in the past – have things always turned out as expected?

People's complexity means that the employer or executive jobseeker can never be 100 percent sure.

This adds in another dimension – **uncertainty**!

Pain + **time** + **uncertainty** can mean one big headache for an employer in trying to hire, not to mention **cost**, which has two dimensions – financial cost and opportunity cost in diverting time and energy away from the day job.

This knowledge gives you, the executive jobseeker, power – the power to influence by making the recruitment process far easier for the employer.

In making the process easier, you have a far better chance of finding and securing the opportunity you want.

This comes from an understanding of the 'hidden market', which I'll discuss later, and going directly to market as part of your executive jobseeker strategy.

The supporting players

So I've talked about the key players in the job market – the employer and the executive jobseeker.

In a football match, it's not just the two teams on the pitch that matter – the referee, timekeeper and medical staff all have an important role to play, too, in ensuring that the game runs smoothly.

There are also supporting players in the executive job market because a gap between employer and jobseeker exists as a result of imperfect information, making it hard to connect.

An employer who has spent time thinking hard about the qualifications, skills, experience and personality of the person she is looking to hire has no guarantee of finding him or her. Where does she look and position herself to get the attention of her target audience?

Similarly, the executive jobseeker might know exactly the type of opportunity he is looking for while being unable to find it.

In this middle ground, we find executive job boards and professional recruiters. Let's talk about both now.

Executive job boards

These have generally superseded press advertising in newspapers and industry publications, although the latter do still exist.

When I started out in recruitment, employers often advertised for talent through adverts in publications such as *The Times.*

These were often expensive and required considerable lead time to go to print. The shelf life was also limited, as today's news is tomorrow's chip paper – but what if the ideal candidate missed today's publication?

With the Internet revolution, things have moved online.

Executive job boards create a market between employer and jobseeker.

For a fee, employers place their job advertisements, and executive jobseekers upload their CVs to apply for positions they're interested in.

Executive job boards work hard on advertising their service through national TV campaigns and other media to ensure they have multiple vacancies and multiple candidates at any one time. It really is a numbers game.

With the click of an e-mail, it's easy to apply for a position through an executive job board. As a result, the quality and relevance of applications for a particular role can be very mixed.

Employers often find themselves wading through multiple CVs to find the one they are looking for, and they then need to run their own recruitment process behind it.

Some might say executive job boards should find the proverbial needle, but the reality is they often just provide the haystack.

Professional recruiters

An alternative to advertising on executive job boards is to use a professional recruitment company.

At the executive level, firms in this space often describe their services as headhunting or search and selection. The implication here is that they aren't just reliant on their database (although they will usually have a rather large one); instead, they go out and find the best candidate given the specific requirements of their client.

As they invest time to do this, they usually charge a proportion of their fee upfront in the form of a retainer. This demonstrates their client's commitment to them and usually means they handle vacancies on a sole agency basis.

This can sometimes prove challenging for executive-level candidates because some less scrupulous firms claim to be the appointed and acting agent – when in fact they are not – to secure a good CV as a carrot to dangle in front of an employer.

On a more positive note, recruitment businesses often specialise in a particular industry (e.g. finance, engineering or aerospace) and therefore have a more detailed understanding of their sector.

They can add more value to the executive jobseeker by advising on current market conditions, specifics on an employer, the interview process and negotiation of an offer. They also give an employer a bit more certainty on a candidate when hiring, as they should meet the candidate before the employer does.

Having taken a brief on the position, they shortlist a selection of the most relevant candidates for their client to interview. Using the previous analogy, they provide a number of needles, having sifted the haystack themselves.

It's important to remember that executive job boards and recruiters are motivated by money. They are commercial organisations with bills to pay and profits to make!

While they represent the interests of their candidates, they often represent the interests of many candidates.

As an executive jobseeker on a very large database, you often have very little control over your own destiny.

There is now an additional way for employers to source talent – through social media channels such as LinkedIn.

Many employers, particularly the larger ones with a resourcing team, are going straight to market by approaching executive jobseekers directly online.

I'll talk more about this later, but for the moment, please remember that never has it been more important to have the right online profile.

To summarise what we've covered so far:

Executive job boards still require the employer to invest a considerable amount of *time* but at a lower *cost* (they provide the haystack).

Recruiters save the employer *time* but at a higher *cost* (they provide a selection of needles). They also provide a bit more *certainty*.

Other executive jobseekers

There's still one player we've not yet discussed who is someone you can never afford to overlook if you're seeking success in the executive job market.

These are your competition – other executive jobseekers who are competing for the same opportunities.

How do executive jobseekers think, feel and act? This is a fairly easy question for you to answer because you are one.

In my experience, executive jobseekers often find their situation extremely uncomfortable.

Often at the top of their profession, though technically brilliant and highly experienced, they come up short when it comes to the skill of finding an executive-level position.

Without a clear understanding of the executive job market and their position in it, executive jobseekers often lack confidence. Worse still, they often suffer from an ever-decreasing level of confidence over time.

Executive jobseekers often lack knowledge of how to successfully position themselves in the executive job market, so they engage third parties to do this for them. They register their CV with executive job boards and agencies – then they wait!

They have very little control over their executive job search apart from checking their inbox and calling their recruitment contacts on a regular basis. This lack of control is a significant factor in causing increased frustration and reduced confidence over time.

If you've ever spoken to an executive recruiter who has said, 'Don't worry, you're still on the radar', I can tell you this often translates as 'You're one of many people we're representing. We'll

14

try not to forget you, but we might just do that. Please stop calling!'

Most executive jobseekers are one of many with profiles on executive job boards and one of many registered with professional recruiters. They are small fish in a very large pond and have limited control over when and how they will be caught – if they are ever caught at all!

Ironically, because this is what most executive jobseekers do, this is what the majority of executive jobseekers think they should do.

But isn't success in the executive job market about standing out from the crowd?

If you do what everyone else is doing and have limited control, which can have a detrimental impact on your confidence, then how is this standing out from the crowd?

Successful executive jobseekers use this knowledge to their advantage and do the opposite. They still sign up to executive job boards and register with recruiters, but that is only a small part of their game – they divert their energy in a different direction!

Exposing the hidden market

This different direction starts with an understanding of the three conversations employers have and relates to the hidden market.

The hidden market is one of the best places to find the executive position you want.

If you've hired staff in the past, you're likely to have had these conversations yourself but may not have consciously thought about them.

Let's look at an example:

John runs his own business and needs to recruit someone into the team.

Conversation one – He asks his peer group, his close circle of associates, to see if they know anyone they could recommend. These are friends or long-standing business associates who have become friends. They are people John knows and trusts.

He'll have a number of conversations like this, and once his personal and trusted network is exhausted, he'll move to conversation two.

Conversation two – Next, John talks to his professional advisors, suppliers and other business contacts. They're not quite in the inner circle, they're not friends or business associates who have become friends, but nonetheless they are people he respects and trusts.

He asks this group whom they know and whom they can potentially recommend. If he gets nowhere, he moves to conversation three.

Conversation three – Finally, John talks to an executive job board about placing an advert or to a professional recruitment company in his sector.

These conversations happen all the time, every day of the week, in all industries and at all levels.

Most executive jobseekers put themselves only in a position to be picked up by conversation three.

If you think of the conversations as ponds, then pond three is the biggest and the most overcrowded. As an executive jobseeker, to maximise your chances of success, you can't afford to just swim in this pond.

Ponds one and two are smaller. There's less competition, and here is actually where John would prefer to fish – not in pond three because that costs him money in advertisement and recruitment fees.

Furthermore, ponds one and two come with an implicit recommendation because the individual being recommended is known by the person making the recommendation. The success of the placement is left less to chance; the candidate is more tried and tested.

Ponds one and two are the hidden market! I'm not saying to discount pond three, but don't rely on it solely. Understanding the existence of the hidden market allows you to position yourself there, too, giving you access to more opportunities with a higher probability of success.

The hidden market also presents an opportunity for the executive jobseeker to create a position that does not yet exist in the mind of the employer – where the employer has no intention to recruit but recruits anyway.

If your organisation were considering expanding into China, if the right individual appeared with the necessary skills and experience, might you bring the decision forward, even if the decision had been intended for a later date?

Although this happens on a less frequent basis, it does happen. When it does, the executive jobseeker in this position has no competition. There are no other candidates in the process, and the opportunity is for the taking.

A quick summary

Understanding the players in the executive job market gives you a distinct advantage over your competition.

Relying solely on executive job boards and professional recruiters leaves the control of your executive job search to someone other than you. While they should be part of your strategy, your emphasis should be on proactively positioning yourself in the hidden market.

THE PSYCHOLOGY OF
EXECUTIVE SUCCESS

In the mad dash to create a perfect CV (there is no such thing, by the way – more on that later), many executive jobseekers miss the most important issue.

What you believe about the job market and your position in it directly correlates to your success.

This chapter will give you a detailed understanding of how beliefs play an important role in your success, challenge your current thought processes and move you to a new position of empowered thinking for positive action.

How most people view the executive job market

In the last chapter, we looked at the key players in the executive job market.

Building on this, let's first explore what the two main players – employers and executive jobseekers – think about their position in the job market.

Employers

- There are lots of great candidates out there; it's a buyer's market.

- Executive jobseekers need us more than we need them and should be grateful for a job.

- We won't hire unless we're absolutely sure; we don't want to take a risk or incur unnecessary cost.

Executive jobseekers

- At the executive level, there aren't many positions out there; it's going to be really, really tough.

- There are lots of other executive jobseekers with just as good or better skills and experience.

- I should be grateful for any executive job I'm offered; I can't afford to be picky.

In summary, employers think, *We have the power*, while executive jobseekers think, *We have little power*. This is not a great position to start from when attacking the executive job market in search of an executive-level position.

The typical executive jobseeker places far too much emphasis on the executive job market and whether it's good or bad; it becomes her main topic of conversation.

I call this the *pinball effect* – the typical executive jobseeker is bounced around emotionally by news reports and things she sees and hears, ultimately things she has no control over and has not personally verified as accurate.

One of the first things I ask a new client is 'What's your opinion on the job market in your industry and at your level?'

Often the response is that 'It's really tough out there' or 'There are very few jobs.'

I then dig deeper and usually ask, 'How do you know that?'

The response is often the following:

'It's all over the news.'

'I know a few people in the same position who have been looking for a long time, and they've found nothing.'

'I'm registered with a few search and selection firms, and they've told me it's tough out there.'

Their beliefs are not their own. Their thinking is not their own. They are a product of their environment and are forced to react to that environment.

This is an ***illusion***!

Take the statements above once more:

'It's all over the news' – does the news always portray an accurate picture of how things really are?

'I know a few people in the same position who have been looking for a long time, and they've found nothing' – are they doing the right things to stand out or copying what everyone else is doing?

'I'm registered with a few search and selection firms, and they've told me it's tough out there' – how big is their client base;

do they understand how the hidden market works; and if they do, would they tell you?

In reality, success in the job market has nothing to do with the job market; it has everything to do with you, the executive jobseeker. Once you grasp this concept, you are free from emotion, you think clearly and you are open to a wider set of options and actions – you are in control of your own destiny. No longer are you *reactive* to other players in the job market; you are *proactive* with total control over your beliefs, your thoughts, your actions and ultimately your success!

Banishing historical beliefs

In Japan, there is a proverb:

'The nail that sticks out gets hammered down.'

It was a regular sight for me to see businessmen, commonly known as 'salarymen', collapsed in exhaustion on the numerous railway and underground platforms that exist all over Tokyo. A salaryman, having finished work late, was often obliged to go drinking with the boss and then missed the last train home. His only option then was a night on the platform before starting the madness all over again the following day.

In Japan, society educates on how to fit in, to set aside individual ambition for the greater good, to just grin and bear it and never make a fuss.

The Japanese also have a somewhat surprising word regarding modern society – *Karōshi*. This word means *death from overwork*! The long hours worked, combined with stress and poor diet, can lead (and sometimes do – after all, they have a word for it) to a heart attack, stroke or sudden death.

Think about our own culture in the Western world. As children, we're wide-eyed and full of hope. We see the world as our adventure playground. However, on arriving at school, we quickly learn that this adventure can sometimes get us into trouble.

Suddenly there are rules we must adhere to and teachers to enforce them. What's more, our classmates begin to introduce and instil further behaviour changes within us. The kid who gets top marks becomes 'teacher's pet', and the one who lands at the bottom of the heap is the 'dunce'.

We learn that it's best not to attract attention to ourselves and are conditioned to blend in. In addition, our education system is built around the concept of learning information to regurgitate as answers to exam questions. We start to take the ideas of others as the only truth and stop thinking for ourselves. Suddenly we've become the nail that doesn't want to stick out for fear of being hammered down.

In the executive job market, to find success, you have to be the nail that's not afraid to stick out. It's the only way to stand out from your competition.

As Walt Disney put it, *'Observe the masses and do the opposite'* – that is, of course, unless you want what the masses have!

Changing your beliefs to change your thought process

We all have a multitude of thoughts, all day every day – even when we're asleep!

However, a thought has no power unless it is supported by a strong belief, which is energy charged with emotion.

What creates an executive jobseeker's urge to action is not just thinking about doing something but the belief-empowered thought supercharged with emotion.

What's the difference between people who think they might do something and those who actually do?

I've worked for myself for the past seven years. I have a number of close friends who work for organisations but talk to me on a regular basis about starting their own business. They are in the 'might' camp – they think about it, but because they don't believe deep down that they'll be successful, their urge to action goes nowhere.

The difference is belief. A true belief is the magic ingredient that determines how you think. A true belief also provides the emotion, which propels a thought into action.

You've probably heard the saying that 'seeing is believing'. Unfortunately, once you've seen it, it's often too late, and the moment or opportunity has passed.

Something many executive jobseekers never see, and hence don't believe in and ultimately take no action to attack, is the hidden market. I can tell you it does exist and is one of the most powerful ways to find an executive position you choose on your terms.

However, until you believe in its existence and are excited by the prospect of accessing it, your thinking will never result in an urge to action, so you'll do nothing about it!

If you believe the executive job market is difficult or that you have little control over your destiny, no matter how much you try to change your thinking, you'll lack the power to take action.

Beliefs charged with emotion, which drive our thinking, are what deliver us our results in life.

If you truly believe in your success in the executive job market so much that you can actually feel it, your success is guaranteed. It's just a matter of time.

Beliefs + Thoughts + Actions = SUCCESS

There really is no place for so-called positive thinking. The effects are only temporary if any exist.

You have to change your beliefs, and to begin with, this requires a focused shift in your conscious mind. As time passes, that shift will be absorbed into your subconscious mind.

There are five things you can start doing today to change your beliefs about the executive job market and your position in it:

1. Take responsibility

2. Beware of self-talk

3. Practice detachment

4. Focus on process, not prize

5. Put yourself on a pedestal

You may already know some of these, but do you really believe in their power? Knowing is not enough to get you to take the necessary action to internalise them as part of who you are.

Let's take a look at each one of the five things listed on the previous page in detail:

1. *Take responsibility*

Human beings are masters of making excuses:

'It's not my fault!'

'It's just how things are!'

'There's nothing I can do!'

'What's the point?'

Most people are responsibility dodgers – but why?

As soon as you take responsibility for something, you become accountable to someone, and there's a risk of failure.

Most people would rather do nothing than risk failing at something. However, they miss the point; through failure we grow as people, and failure is a training ground for success.

In an organisation, any failure is usually shared. However senior you've become, there's usually another set of shoulders to share the weight or at least someone else to blame.

In the executive job market, you're on your own, and what's more, it's personal – it's your life, after all.

This is why it's tempting to leave your success in the hands of executive job boards or recruiters. If things don't happen for you, well, it wasn't up to you, was it?

You have to get past the fear of failure and understand that failure is just part of the process of finding your next executive position.

I've met some amazing candidates in my time in recruitment who have gone on to have fantastic careers and have reached the top of their game. They all have one thing in common – none of them has ever been offered every single executive job he or she went for; they all failed at some point along the way.

Furthermore, we often find it easier to be accountable to others than to be accountable to ourselves.

Imagine the scenario – it's a cold and wet winter evening, and you're due at the gym for your Tuesday night class.

If you've agreed to meet your friend there, you're far more likely to go because you're accountable to someone else. To get out of it would require an uncomfortable text or an awkward phone call.

If you were planning to go on your own, how easy is it to make an excuse and convince yourself that it's OK to forget it tonight? As human beings, we do this all the time!

Take a moment to think about the last time you decided not to do something and how you justified it to yourself.

I still do this, but the difference is that I now catch myself doing it; it's in my conscious mind and no longer in a blind spot. As I work at this, I'm forming a positive habit that will ultimately live in my subconscious.

The successful executive jobseeker understands this and knows that finding her next executive position is ***totally her own responsibility***.

While I was working with Clive, he relocated from Switzerland to Spain. In the run-up to the relocation, he stopped taking the action we'd agreed he would take and deviated from his personal executive jobseeker plan (more on how to construct one of these later).

I quizzed him on why, and he explained that he was busy with getting ready to move. However he dressed it up, he was making an excuse. He had lost control of his executive job search.

I spoke with him about this and told him he had to make a decision.

If Clive made the conscious decision to postpone his executive job search while he relocated, that was fine – his responsibility, his decision, and under his control.

That was what Clive decided to do. He took time out for two weeks before coming back with beliefs, thoughts and actions intact.

What you believe is your choice; how you think is your choice; how you act is your choice – you're in total control of your destiny.

2. Beware of self-talk

Linked closely to taking responsibility is understanding the power of self-talk.

Self-talk is the little voice inside our heads that questions us, doubts us and generally can be a complete pain in the neck!

It's also more than that, being the words we use in our everyday communications and conversations.

Let's look at two executive jobseekers – Mia and Jim. Both have exactly the same background and have found themselves on the executive job market through redundancy.

Mia's self-talk is full of 'I can....I will....', whereas Jim's is full of 'I can't....I might....I'll try.' From this information alone, on whom would you place money to be the first person to find an executive position?

You see, self-talk can either be debilitating or empowering, and the best news is that it's absolutely up to you how you choose to talk to yourself – it just takes practice.

Taking responsibility and using empowering *self-talk* is a conscious shift in behaviour. Once internalised, it starts to change beliefs, thoughts and actions.

There are two extremely powerful techniques that serve to support this shift.

Peer pressure – People close to you (family members or friends) are a great form of support and also accountability. Be honest and open with them about your current situation, and explain to them that you are taking *full* responsibility for moving forward.

Ban excuses, and ask them to tell you if and when you make them; you'll soon stop using them.

Similarly ban debilitating self-talk – no more 'can't', no more 'might' and definitely no more 'try' – 'try' is just one step away from saying 'won't'!

Thinking journal – Start a diary or what I prefer to call a thinking journal that documents not only everything you did or didn't do but what was going on in your head at the time – what were you thinking and feeling?

The more frequent and detailed, the better – it's a log of everything that you currently are and bring to the table in everyday life. This provides clues to changes you can and will make to be so much more.

Your thinking journal is personal to you and is *extremely powerful*. The act of documenting your innermost thoughts and feelings brings them from your subconscious into your conscious mind.

You start to see on paper the excuses and disempowering self-talk that are holding you back.

Your thinking journal acts as a mirror to the real you and all you bring to bear in the executive job market. Now, in your conscious mind, you have the power to change.

Documenting and observing your behaviour in this way will help you move forward.

3. Practice detachment

As an executive jobseeker, it is crucial that you detach yourself from the past and also the future.

Have you ever heard yourself say something like 'Wasn't it great when...?' or 'I'll be happy when...'? We all do this all the time, which means we miss the very moment we're in and the only thing we can control.

The past is gone, and the future will take care of itself – *leave the past alone and forget the future!*

The fact that an interview didn't go well last week doesn't mean that your interview today will be the same!

Don't confuse this with not learning from the past or with getting feedback from previous interviews. These things, too, are hugely important to learn and grow from. The point here is that what happened yesterday doesn't mean the same will or must happen today – each moment is full of new possibility and opportunity.

Similarly, detaching from what may happen tomorrow releases you to focus on what's important today, and in reality, that's all that matters – what you choose to do now is the only thing you can ever control.

Everything is independent and in isolation – there is no connection between you last week and you today, or you today and you next month – the only connection is the connection you make in your head.

Being present opens you up to opportunities that might be right in front of you – opportunities you probably would have otherwise missed!

4. Focus on process, not prize

Most of us would probably like to be fitter than we are, and some of us may attend a gym.

Whether you go to the gym or not is your decision – the following story, though, will help to explain why focusing on process and not outcome is so important in the executive job market.

Let's meet Tom. Tom wants to get fit. He's joined a gym, he's bought the health and fitness magazines, and he's imagining what life will be like when he has the physique he wants.

He goes to the gym three times a week, but every time he comes home, he's disappointed. Looking in the mirror, his muscles don't seem to have grown, and he doesn't feel any fitter. Pretty soon he stops going, stays home and gets depressed. He wonders, *What's the point? When I was going, it made no difference anyway!*

Tom was focused on the **prize**; he was focused on the outcome alone.

Joining the gym was the easy part – the hard work then starts. Because Tom didn't get the results he wanted immediately, he became despondent and gave up.

If he'd only focused on the **process**, remained detached from outcomes and trained regularly in a disciplined and diligent way, his end goal would have taken care of itself – he'd have achieved the physique and fitness he so desired.

We can't really blame Tom. In a world of instant gratification, we all want results right here, right now.

Tom had an end goal in mind, which is massively important, but his timescale for achieving it was unrealistic. He was obsessed with the goal and ultimately gave up on the process.

The same is true for the executive jobseeker. Focusing on the outcome of securing an executive position can damage your ability to find and secure the very executive job you are looking for – it takes away your energy and enthusiasm.

Understanding the importance of time and your personal time frame for finding an executive job in your sector and at your level leads to realistic expectations.

The road to finding that next position is paved with rejection. You will not be offered every executive job you interview for, and it won't always be your day.

This is just part of the process. Remember, you only need one executive job – rejection along the way is experience gained that helps you get the position meant for you. The process builds character.

The successful executive jobseeker realises this and accepts it from the outset – it's all just part of the game.

As Rudyard Kipling advised in his famous poem and at the start of this book:

'If you can keep your head while all around you are losing theirs...!'

Accept rejection as part of the experience, and keep your head for next time.

The successful executive jobseeker knows that it's not about finding the job but rather about running a *process*, which results in the desired outcome taking care of itself.

5. Put yourself on a pedestal

Success in the executive job market has nothing to do with the executive job market or with employers, professional recruiters, executive job boards or anything else – it has *everything to do with you*.

You have the ability to participate in the executive job market when and how you choose.

Your success centres on you and starts with you understanding your environment, your beliefs and your thought processes.

You then choose how to participate through your personal executive jobseeker plan, which we'll cover soon, supported by the skills and techniques that feed into your process.

By taking responsibility, changing your self-talk, detaching from the past and future, and focusing on process alone, you put yourself at the centre of your executive job search – you, and no one else, are on the pedestal!

Putting yourself on a pedestal moves you from a *reactive* position bounced around by the actions of others (the *pinball effect*) to a *proactive* position in which you are in full control.

In reality, the employer doesn't have the power – *you do!*

And finally...

What you believe, how you think and what actions you take, determine the results you get in life.

The *law of attraction* is built on the premise that what happens to you was ultimately attracted by you.

What you believe, think and do creates energy, and this energy attracts similar energy.

Your brain is one big search engine – a bit like Google. Type in *other people are better than I am* or *the executive job market is difficult*, and Google will throw out information in line with your thoughts.

Your brain is the same – garbage in leads to garbage out.

Likewise, empowered beliefs, thoughts and actions result in more of the same. The universe knows – so be careful what you wish for!

A quick summary

What you believe and think is *everything*. Understanding that success in the executive job market has *nothing to do* with the executive job market and *everything to do* with you is a key difference between most executive jobseekers and the successful executive jobseeker.

Thinking and acting differently from your competition sets you apart from them, and moving from *reactive* to *proactive* is not only empowering but also self-fulfilling.

YOUR PLAN OF ATTACK

Any successful journey requires a destination in mind from the outset.

Rarely do we leave home, get in our car and just drive. Usually we are heading somewhere; there is purpose to our journey.

Even when we have a destination in mind, we still need confidence in our directions. Without clear directions, we're likely to end up confused, lost and miles from home!

It's exactly the same in your journey through the executive job market.

Now with strong foundations, a detailed understanding of the executive job market environment, and the psychology for executive success, it's time to devise your plan of attack.

In this chapter, you'll learn how to construct a personal executive jobseeker plan, which will form the framework for everything you do.

The importance of planning

Whether you are currently in an executive job and looking for your next career move or out of work and keen to find your next executive position, you need a personal executive jobseeker plan.

Finding an executive role is a business in itself. You are now the managing director of your own company called Finding an Executive Position Limited.

There are no employees in your organisation, and the buck stops with you – success or failure is 100 percent your responsibility.

At the heart of any successful business is a clear and concise plan that everyone in the organisation is aligned to – it ensures clarity of direction and unity in purpose.

Many senior executives spend a large proportion of their time planning. It's a way to justify and monitor expenditure and to check on progress and performance.

In business they do this all the time, but when it comes to their own executive job search, they leave the chance of success to a series of haphazard and uncoordinated actions over which they have little or no control.

Don't get me wrong; you might find an executive position quickly without documenting your personal executive jobseeker plan. I hope you do, provided that it's the opportunity you really want and not something you're simply grabbing because it's the only thing available. Don't eat the scraps from under the table!

There is something very special about the job market, which is one of the principal reasons that spending time constructing a well-thought-out plan and then sticking to it is of paramount importance.

Looking for an executive position is emotional!

Protecting your emotions is fundamental to your success in the executive job market.

A personal executive jobseeker plan removes this emotion. You have a plan, and your job is to stick to it no matter what. It's all about running a process and being disciplined and diligent in following your plan each and every day.

Your plan is written to deliver your end goal of finding an executive position in a realistic and defined time period. In knowing this, you can disengage yourself from the outcome and the emotion that comes with it, while trusting that you'll ultimately secure the executive position you want.

Executive jobseekers often suffer from an illusion that the harder they work, the more success they will have and the sooner it will come. Nothing could be further from the truth.

Thinking about the executive job market and looking for a position morning, noon and night is a common failure of most executive jobseekers.

They focus on nothing else; it becomes their sole purpose for being. They check their e-mail constantly and review the executive job boards multiple times each day. There's no downtime, and eventually they burn out physically and emotionally.

Your plan protects you from this emotion; it stops you from constantly thinking about the executive job market and maintains your mental well-being.

The three stages of planning

A personal executive jobseeker plan has three elements.

Destination – Where are you going, and how long will it take to get there?

Direction – How do you get there?

Discipline – How are you going to ensure that you stay on course, remain focused, and keep your energy level up?

Stage one – Destination

It all starts with defining your destination – defining your end *goal* and the *time* it will take to get there.

To define your goal requires that you answer three questions. Don't be limited by disempowering thoughts; whether current opportunities are in line with your answers is irrelevant.

Remember, you are no longer reacting to what's out there; you're instead defining where you're going. That's a huge difference!

1. Why are you looking for a job?

People experience *push* and *pull* factors when making a decision to enter the executive job market.

An example of a push factor is redundancy; you were pushed to leave your current position as your role ceased to exist.

An example of a pull factor could be excitement at the prospect of entering a different industry sector at a senior level – the grass looks greener, and you're keen to apply the expertise you've gained in your current sector in a different environment.

Sometimes push and pull factors can be one and the same – they combine to reinforce an urge to action and as such can have more power.

For example, you believe your skills are underutilised in your current role (the push) and have seen an executive position advertised where you can put your skills and experience to better use (the pull).

To uncover your push and pull factors, take a moment now to complete the exercise below.

Exercise one

Start with a blank piece of paper with a line down the middle. Above the left column, write **push**, and above the right, write **pull**.

Time yourself for two minutes and start writing everything that comes into your head as fast as you can. Don't stop and think – just write, and keep writing until the time is up!

What do you notice? What does this tell you about yourself? Are there patterns or common themes to your push and pull factors?

Often, push factors can be negative whereas pull factors can have a more positive spin.

Which do you think an executive recruiter or a future employer will want to hear more about when it comes to an interview?

Please keep this exercise; you'll need it again shortly.

2. Who do you want to work for?

If you had the choice – and remember now, you *do* have the choice – who would you like to work for?

The *who* can be a company or a type of individual or both – what's important is that you define it clearly and concisely.

Think about what size of organisation, what sector and in what location. Be cognisant of your current skills and experience and where they may fit best.

If you have experience in manufacturing, then other manufacturing businesses could be a good starting point. If you've previously worked for large organisations, it could make sense to target big businesses first. To help answer this question, take a moment now to complete the exercise below.

Exercise two

Take a blank piece of paper and draw three large circles. In each circle, write one of the following – organisation, person and location.

Take two minutes on each stage – time yourself and work as fast as you can. Try not to think; just write down what comes into your head. Don't question or analyse what you are writing – just write.

Organisation – List organisations that you think you'd like to work for. It doesn't matter where they're based or whether they're hiring; it's about documenting organisations you have an affinity with or an interest in. Write them down!
(An example here could be Virgin.)

Person – List people for whom you'd like to work. Be specific and name them. Write as many down as possible during the timed period.
(An example here could be Sir Richard Branson.)

Location – Write down geographical areas you're prepared to

work in. Again, be specific. If London is your choice, determine where, specifically, in London you'd like to work. This will be influenced by your preferred distance to commute and willingness to relocate nationally or internationally.

Please keep this exercise. You'll need it again shortly.

3. What type of job do you want?

Similarly, what type of job do you want? What skills will you be using, and what types of responsibilities will you have?

Remember that employers will be looking for relevant qualifications or experience. You're less likely to walk into an opportunity to do something you have no knowledge of or experience doing before.

There will be skills and experience you have *now* and those that you wish to develop in the *future*.

Exercise three

Take another blank piece of paper and draw a line down the middle. On the left-hand side at the top, write **now**, and on the right, write **future**.

Under **now**, write down the skills and experience you have obtained to date, and under **future**, the skills and experience you're looking to develop as your career progresses.

Time yourself for two minutes, and start writing everything that comes into your head as fast as you can. Don't stop and think – just write and keep writing until the time is up.

Please keep this exercise. You'll need it again shortly.

By thinking about these three questions and doing the exercises, you've gone a long way towards defining your destination and have done something that most executive jobseekers will never do.

You may have found the exercises quite simplistic, but remember what Leonardo da Vinci said: *'Simplicity is the ultimate sophistication.'*

If you glossed over the exercises (we all do it), please go back and invest the time required to do them properly; it's important.

Some of my previous clients found these exercises difficult at first. If you need any additional help or support, please feel free to get in touch via my website: https://careercodex.com

Not only does knowing where you are going focus your attack on the executive job market, but it means that in any dialogue with a professional recruiter or potential employer, you will be more focused and convincing.

You're better equipped to explain why you want to work for a particular organisation.

Remember, too, the *law of attraction*. When you think about and subsequently focus on what you really want, you create energy, which serves to attract the very thing you're after.

So now let's take each exercise and analyse it to clearly define your destination and executive jobseeker *goal.* Take the three pieces of paper you used to complete the exercises.

1. Why?
Exercise one – *Push* and *pull* factors.

The trick here is to focus on the positive, which can be and often are the pull factors. Circle two or three things that are the most important to you.

2. Who?
Exercise two – *Organisation*, *person* and *location*.

What do these tell you about your preferred next move?

Organisation – What are the similar factors among the organisations you've named? Is there a common theme in terms of size, sector or something else?

Person – Of the people you've named, what are two or three things they have in common?

(The leader of the organisation often sets the company culture, so getting specific here further defines the organisation you want to work for.)

Location – This is often the easiest to define. Which locations, specifically, do you want to work in? Even if you're internationally flexible, you have to focus your attention somewhere.

3. What?
Exercise three – *Now* and *future*.

Of your current skills, which are your strongest? Which are you most confident in, and where can you demonstrate achievement? Focus on only two or three, and circle them.

Similarly, looking at the list of skills you'd like to develop, which is the most important? Settle on just one, and circle it.

Pulling these together, you define your executive jobseeker *goal*.

For example:

I (insert name here) will find a new challenge that better utilises my skills and experience.

I will work for a large aerospace organisation that is passionate and entrepreneurial and based in Hamburg or Berlin.

I will utilise my executive leadership and project management skills and will also have the opportunity to gain a more in-depth knowledge of the German culture and language.

You need to sense check your end goal to ensure that the sum of the parts is a realistic and possible whole.

For example, if there are no large aerospace organisations in Hamburg or Berlin, you may need to go back to the drawing board.

Your goal is so important; it aligns everything else in your personal executive jobseeker plan to deliver it.

It enables you to do the following:

- Be selective in whom you approach.

- Deliver a consistent message.

- Remove distraction through focus.

Your goal sits at the top of your one-page personal executive jobseeker plan and is something you read at the start of every day.

Now that you've defined your *goal*, the next step is to look at the *time* it will take to get there. *Time* is the other important but often overlooked factor in defining your destination.

Setting realistic timescales relevant to your industry and seniority level is key.

Time has two elements that you need to consider – *calendar time* and *investment time*.

Calendar time – how long it typically takes people in your industry and at your level to move in the executive job market.

If you are a chief executive officer (CEO), regardless of your industry sector, it's likely to take you a reasonable amount of time. Opportunities at the top of any organisation are few and far between.

If you set unrealistic expectations on the time it will take you to find your next executive position, what do you think this will do to you emotionally?

If you estimate a month based on hope but the market indicates six months, how empowered will you be if you don't hit your personal target? How will it help you in the remaining five months? The short answer is that it won't, so don't set yourself up to fail from the outset.

Setting a realistic timescale is important; it helps to protect you emotionally and also allows you to budget.

If you're currently unemployed, your personal savings or a redundancy payoff will last only for so long. Dividing your financial reserves by the time you estimate it will take you to find your next executive position tells you what you can spend each month.

Financial pressure shows up as emotional pressure, and desperation to find a job can creep in if you're not careful. Focusing on outcome and not process can be damaging and may show up in all of your communications. Remember, it's process, not prize, for good reason.

If you're not sure how long it will take you to secure your next role, find out by asking questions.

- Who do you know who has successfully moved positions at a similar level in a similar industry recently?

- Talk to specialist recruiters who work in the industry each and every day. They will be able to provide some useful insight.

- Get involved with specialist groups on LinkedIn; start discussions and ask questions of other group members. It's a great way to start a conversation and could actually lead to your next executive opportunity.

A quick word of caution: I advised earlier that you be careful what you believe. Trade in fact and not opinion; place value on real-life examples of recent moves over someone's opinion of how long it might take. The former carries much more weight.

Investment time – how much time you can dedicate to your executive job search each week.

If you're currently in full-time employment, you'll have less time than someone between positions. It's therefore likely to take you longer because you have less time to invest each week. On the flip side, though, you're likely to be under less financial pressure.

Taking responsibility for your executive job search and taking a proactive approach, which includes exploring the hidden market, requires more time investment on your part. Factor in how much time you have each week. Calendar and investment time are related. If you know from your enquiries that it's likely to take you four to six months to find your next executive position (calendar time), then the more investment time you can dedicate to your executive job search, the more probable it is that you'll secure a position in four months instead of six.

Time sits under *goal* at the top of your one-page personal executive jobseeker plan. The two combine to form your **destination statement**.

Here's an example destination statement.

Goal
I (insert name here) will find a new challenge that better utilises my skills and experience.

I will work for a large aerospace organisation that is passionate and entrepreneurial and based in Hamburg or Berlin.

I will utilise my executive leadership and project management skills and will also have the opportunity to gain a more in-depth knowledge of the German culture and language.

Time
I will dedicate 37.5 hours to my job search each week – 7.5 hours each day (Monday to Friday) from 8:00 a.m. to 5:00 p.m. (One hour for lunch and two 15-minute breaks).

How does your destination statement look on paper? Is it realistic and something you can and will commit to? How do you feel? Are you excited and confident in what you've written?

If the answer is *yes* – fantastic! You are ready to proceed to the next stage. But if your answer is anything other than a resounding *yes*, why is that?

Getting this stage right is absolutely critical, and time invested here is time well spent. What you document is everything; it's where you'll direct your energy, emotion and effort, and it's where you'll find success.

If you need to repeat the process, that's fine; go back and do the exercises again – you'll know when *yes* is really *yes*. You'll not only know it; you'll feel it!

Stage two – Direction

The second stage of planning is to define your direction, which is another essential component of your personal executive jobseeker plan.

This is essentially what you will do and when you will do it – it's the day-to-day activity that gets you from **A** to **B**.

A is where you are now, and **B** is the place you've just defined in your destination statement.

It's essential that you have a balanced portfolio of activity that you stick to in line with the investment time period you've now defined.

Variety is important to keep you engaged and motivated. Another reason it is important is that the people in a position to hire you or introduce you to the hidden market often like to be approached in different ways.

Many executive jobseekers I've interviewed proudly tell me how they are surfing the executive job boards morning, noon and night. Not only are they missing the point and doing the wrong thing, but also they're doing far too much of it!

Professional athletes understand the power of rest. They exert their muscles and then rest to allow their bodies to repair and grow. This is how they get faster, get stronger and avoid injury.

Executive jobseekers rarely get this and think working around the clock at all hours of the day and night will increase their chances of success. Injury for an executive jobseeker is loss of motivation and loss of confidence. As athletes know, one of the best ways to avoid injury is to get proper rest.

To maintain your emotional well-being, you need to set your start and finish times.

Outside of these hours, you do nothing relating to your executive job search; you go and do something else, ideally something you enjoy with your loved ones.

More effort might feel good today, but it will likely lead to less effort tomorrow.

Remember that the weekends are still the weekends. Don't be tempted to surf the Internet, check your e-mail or do anything related to finding your next executive position. Instead, use this time for things you enjoy, including family, hobbies and interests.

Remember that your executive jobseeker plan is personal to you. The daily activities you define will be specific to your *goal* and the *time* you have available.

Your personal executive jobseeker plan, as you've seen, clarifies the destination in the form of your destination statement.

To arrive at your destination, you need to take diligent and consistent action. This action is a balanced portfolio of activity that you undertake within your investment time and will lead you from A to B within the calendar time period you've defined.

For each day you commit to participating in the executive job market, you need a daily action plan.

Your daily action plan can be the same each day, or it can vary from one day to the next. It's important that, once you define it and commit it to paper, you stick to it no matter what!

On the next page you will see an example of a daily action plan. Your plan may look similar or completely different. What's important is that you have one.

If your investment time is less each day, you may decide to allocate certain activities to a particular day; it's really up to you.

For the moment, don't worry too much about the individual activities and what they should or shouldn't be. I appreciate that some of the terms may be unfamiliar at this stage – we'll cover these later in **process**.

Just know that you'll need a daily action plan. You can always come back and fill in the details later.

Time	Activity
8:00 a.m.– 8:30 a.m.	Read my plan and visualise my goal.
8:30 a.m.– 10:45 a.m.	Networking events / meetings.
10:45 a.m.– 11:00 a.m.	**Tea / coffee break.**
11:00 a.m.– 12:00 p.m.	Telephone calls to professional recruiters / employers / marketmakers.
12:00 p.m.– 1:00 p.m.	Target letters to organisations.
1:00 p.m.– 2:00 p.m.	**Lunch and physical activity.**
2:00 p.m.– 3:00 p.m.	Work on my personal branding / online presence.
3:00 p.m.– 3:15 p.m.	**Tea / coffee break.**
3:15 p.m.– 4:30 p.m.	Review executive job boards and online applications.
4:30 p.m.– 5:00 p.m.	Catch-up time & check e-mail.

In this example, does anything jump out?

There are three important points to notice:

- The day is set up to do the difficult things first. It's often harder to meet people and make telephone calls than it is to sit in front of the computer. Do whatever you find the most difficult first.

- If you're currently out of work and dedicated solely to finding an executive position, make sure you get out of the house at least once a day, and do it as early as you can. Networking events are great for this; they often start early and get you talking and engaging with others, which is a great way to build confidence and set up the rest of your day.

- E-mail can be both a blessing and a curse; what's certain is that it can be a huge distraction and as such should be left to check until the end of the day. Writing and responding to e-mail is not the most important thing you should be doing in the executive job market, but if you're not careful and fall into the same trap as your competition, it can fast become the only thing you do.

Stage three – Discipline

So far we've looked at defining your **destination** – your executive position goal and the time it will take you to get to it – in your destination statement.

We've also discussed **direction** – the daily activity you need to take to reach your destination.

The final stage of successful planning focuses on **discipline**.

Think back to your school exams. You probably had a clear goal in mind to get good grades.

To get good grades, if you were anything like me, you probably put together a revision timetable. This allocated time throughout the week to focus on one particular subject at a time, with all subjects covered in equal measure.

I spent ages on my revision timetable. It would be colour coded and would be positioned proudly on my wall above my desk, which would be piled high with files and books.

Putting the revision timetable together was the easy part; sticking to it proved more difficult. I would find myself going off track, discarding my first plan and wasting a few more hours carefully crafting a new one – time I should have spent actually revising.

You see, best-laid plans need discipline to ensure they are carried out.

Creating a plan that you don't follow is a pointless exercise – a destination with direction that lacks discipline has little chance of success.

To find success in the executive job market, it's your personal responsibility to stick to your plan every day, to be diligently disciplined in the activities you've set for yourself to carry out.

Your job is to follow and trust in your plan detached from the outcome of finding an executive position, knowing that the direction you have set for yourself will get you to your destination.

Maintaining discipline is achieved through a personal support system, which has four key components:

1. Peer pressure

2. Measurement

3. Rewards

4. Self-evaluation

I'll cover each of these in turn.

Peer pressure

I talked earlier about taking responsibility and how it's often easier to be accountable to others than to be accountable to ourselves.

If you tell someone you're going to do something, you're more likely to do it. But if you agree to do something with someone else, you're almost certain to do it – such is the power of peer pressure!

This starts with empowering the people around you and bringing them on the journey with you. Share your personal executive jobseeker plan with your nearest and dearest – they're there to support you and also to hold you accountable.

Communicating your plan to those around you at the outset removes negative emotions such as resentment and guilt. Your family and friends will know when you're active in the executive job market and not to disturb you. They'll also know that you have a finish time when they'll receive your full attention.

Searching for an executive position, whether you are currently in employment or not, you're not alone.

Even if you don't currently know anyone in your situation, such people exist and are likely to be going to the same places and doing things similar to those you do.

Striking up a conversation and teaming up with someone else to provide support and hold each other accountable can be mutually beneficial, motivating and rewarding.

My aikido course in Japan was tough. All of us had good days and bad days. There were some who moaned constantly and drained the energy of the group, in contrast to others who were a source of inspiration and energy.

I teamed up with an Israeli guy named Ronen. We both fell into the inspiration and energy camp but knew that it wouldn't all be plain sailing. Ronen was a keen diver, and we borrowed the term 'buddy system' to keep each other going when times got tough.

During some of the most difficult classes, we would shout this out to each other, and it kept us going – we never quit.

Find a buddy, but be careful whom you pick. Those who make excuses and fail to take personal responsibility for their own situation will drain your time and energy.

Find the right buddy, though, and you'll both gain much from the experience.

Measurement

The physical action of measuring what you do and ticking off activities once you complete them is a fantastic tool to support your discipline.

What gets measured typically gets done. It's very easy to get distracted, but when a target is attached to any activity, distraction can take a back seat.

Measurement also allows for comparison, serving to generate healthy competition from day to day or week to week, for increased productivity in the time allocated to each activity in your personal executive jobseeker plan.

It's also a great tool to identify early on where activity levels are dropping off as a means to uncover the reasons sooner rather than later.

On the next page, you will find an example of a daily action plan with measurement.

Daily Action Plan with Measurement			
Time	Activity	No.	✓
8:00 a.m.– 8:30 a.m.	Read my plan and visualise my goal.		
8:30 a.m.– 10:45 a.m.	Networking events / meetings *(target of 1 per day).*	1	
10:45 a.m.– 11:00 a.m.	**Tea / coffee break.**		
11:00 a.m.– 12:00 p.m.	Telephone calls to professional recruiters / employers / marketmakers *(target of 6 decision makers).*	6	
12:00 p.m.– 1:00 p.m.	Target letters to organisations *(target of 3 sent).*	3	
1:00 p.m.– 2:00 p.m.	**Lunch and physical activity.**		
2:00 p.m.– 3:00 p.m.	Work on my personal branding / online presence *(target on LinkedIn of 5 new connections and 3 posts in relevant groups).*	5 3	
3:00 p.m.– 3:15 p.m.	**Tea / coffee break.**		
3:15 p.m.– 4:30 p.m.	Review executive job boards and online applications *(target of 3 applications).*	3	
4:30 p.m.– 5:00 p.m.	Catch-up time & check e-mail (self-evaluation of performance using my thinking journal).		

Rewards

The ultimate reward for following your personal executive jobseeker plan is finding and securing the executive position you want.

Targets set for activity levels that create incentives in the form of rewards can be very powerful in maintaining discipline and reinforcing positive behaviour.

It's not so much about what the reward is; it's the fact that you achieved and then experienced the reward. It could be as simple as arranging to meet a close friend for dinner if you exceed the number of decision makers reached in any one day.

Self-evaluation

This is probably the most important aspect of maintaining discipline.

Remember that success in the executive job market is about taking personal responsibility and has ***everything to do with you***. You choose how and when you participate in the executive job market and take full responsibility for everything that happens or fails to happen.

You've already been introduced to the concept of a thinking journal. Remember, this is where you record not only everything you did or didn't do as part of your executive job search, but also what you were thinking and feeling at the time.

Completed each and every day, this becomes a powerful window to see into yourself and the way you think.

If there are problems with your discipline or disempowering excuses, justifications, assumptions or expectations creeping into your self-talk, this is where you'll uncover them. This links closely with measurement. If you are missing targets or not sticking to your plan, the reasons will likely show up in your thinking journal.

For example:

Jane notices that last Wednesday, she was late starting her daily activities and achieved only 50 percent of the calls she was targeted to make. Why was that?

Going back to her thinking journal, she asks, 'What excuses did I make? What was I justifying? What stories was I telling myself to let me off the hook?'

Her journal says that she was tired – well, why was that? Looking to the night before, she notices that she stayed up late to watch a movie.

This reduced her ability to focus the following day and had a detrimental impact on her productivity.

Building on the example above, having identified the excuse of being tired and linking this back to the disempowering behaviour of staying up late, Jane introduces a rule to protect herself moving forward:

I will go to bed every night at 10:00 p.m. so that I am ready and fresh for the following day.

This rule is now added to her personal executive jobseeker plan. As you conduct your own self-evaluation each day, you will add more rules to your personal executive jobseeker plan that serve to protect and reinforce your discipline.

Through self-evaluation, you work on the most important thing in your success or failure in the job market – *you!*

Pulling all of the elements of this chapter together, you are now in a position to put together your own personal executive jobseeker plan.

To help you, I've included a sample personal executive jobseeker plan on the next page.

My Personal Executive Jobseeker Plan
(insert your name)
Destination – (where I'm going)

Destination statement

Goal

- I (insert name here) will find a new challenge that better utilises my skills and experience.
- I will work for a large aerospace organisation that is passionate and entrepreneurial and based in Hamburg or Berlin.
- I will utilise my executive leadership and project management skills and will also have the opportunity to gain a more in-depth knowledge of the German culture and language.

Time

- I will dedicate 37.5 hours to my job search each week – 7.5 hours each day (Monday to Friday) from 8:00 a.m. to 5:00 p.m. (One hour for lunch and two 15-minute breaks).

Direction – (how I'll get there)

Insert
Daily Action Plan with Measurement
from **page 51** here.

Discipline – (how I'll stay on track)

Rules *(continually build on these through the process of self-evaluation).*

1. I will stick to my designated hours and never work on weekends.
2. I will complete my thinking journal throughout the day and document everything that I am thinking and feeling.
3. I will go to bed every night at 10:00 p.m. so that I am ready and fresh for the following day.

A quick summary

Your personal executive jobseeker plan defines your goal and the series of steps and actions needed to reach this goal over a defined and realistic period of time.

A defined destination, clear direction and the discipline to ensure you stay on course are essential to your success in the executive job market.

Success is all about what you choose to do, and your personal executive jobseeker plan sets the framework and rules on when and how you will participate in the executive job market.

Your sole objective is to stick to your personal executive jobseeker plan and work at it diligently each and every day.

Your personal executive jobseeker plan is the framework for everything you do in the executive job market; it's the toolbox for success. The **process**, which we'll move to now, provides the detailed toolkit that supports the individual activities in your plan.

– THE PROCESS –
EIGHT STEPS TO SUCCESS

You are now equipped with a detailed understanding of the executive job market environment, the ability to think differently from other executive jobseekers and the tools necessary to put together your own personal executive jobseeker plan.

You are now ready to proactively attack the executive job market on your terms. Much of what we've covered so far may be very new and in some cases surprising to you.

In what follows, you will see familiar terminology that people normally associate with navigating the executive job market. Although the terminology might sound familiar, I can promise you that the approach is very different and builds on the solid foundations we've covered thus far.

The following eight steps will guide you successfully through the executive job market and position you ahead of your competition every step of the way:

1. The Super Executive CV / Résumé

2. Cover Letters

3. Getting in Front of Decision Makers

4. The First-Class Executive Interview

5. The Online Executive

6. Effective Executive Networking

7. Innovate to Stay Ahead

8. Handling the Offer & Negotiation Stage

Let's begin...!

STEP ONE:

THE SUPER EXECUTIVE CV / RÉSUMÉ

A CV / résumé is an essential requirement for any executive jobseeker but is only a small part of any successful executive job search strategy.

Many executive jobseekers spend too much time writing, assessing and rewriting their CV in the hope that with each amendment, they'll move closer to the executive job they want – this is a common and significant mistake!

There is no such thing as a perfect CV; much depends on the reader and what they're looking for – something that can never be 100 percent certain.

Why is it, then, that so many executive jobseekers spend an excessive amount of time tweaking and amending their CV in search of a pot of gold that exists only in their imagination?

On the flip side, spending too little time on your CV is a recipe for disaster. It's often the first opportunity for an executive recruiter or employer to make a judgment on you and your experience.

As there are lots and lots of other CVs out there in the executive job market, time and effort making your CV stand out is time well spent.

It really is all about balance – spend enough time to make your CV as good as it can be, and then do something with it.

Whatever you do, don't chase perfection and fall into the trap of taking no action at all.

Key principles of a super executive CV

Before getting into detail, let's take a look at some key principles and things to take note of before writing your CV.

Purpose

Your CV has one purpose and one purpose only, and that's to get you an interview; it's to get you in front of a decision maker who has the power to offer you a job. It's not your life history, and it's definitely not every bit of experience you've ever had, carefully crafted into pages and pages of bland and uninspiring text! Think of it another way, using a real-life analogy.

The weekend arrives, and you decide to go and see a movie. You haven't the time to see every movie that's ever been released, and you don't want to make a mistake, pick the wrong film and waste your Saturday night. So what do you do beforehand to decide what to watch?

Executive recruiters and employers think in exactly the same way – they can't meet everyone who applies to them; they need a filter, and that filter is your CV.

Getting back to the movies; to decide what film to see, you're likely to read a review or watch a trailer. These are snippets of information, digested in two minutes or so to help you make a decision.

Your CV is exactly the same; it's the highlights of you, the executive jobseeker, packaged clearly and concisely so you're the one who gets picked. Your CV is the trailer that secures you the interview.

Any trailer must have three elements:

It *Must* stand out.

It *Must* be memorable.

It *Must* have impact.

These are the three Ms of creating a powerful CV.

The two waves!

Although having the right people in a business is possibly the most important thing for the success of any organisation, it is often given low priority.

As previously discussed, recruiting can be one big *pain* for employers. They have limited *time* to dedicate to it and would prefer to use this time running their organisation and making money.

As such, employers and professional recruiters read CVs in two waves – your aim is to make it to wave two.

When I say 'read', I don't actually mean read – I mean scan or skim. They haven't the time to read every line or paragraph. They're searching for something that stands out.

In reality, your CV may get only 15 seconds of airtime.

You have 15 seconds to make an impression!

Wave one – Your CV is skimmed and placed in one of three piles.

1. YES – looks interesting; will read a bit more later and likely invite for interview.

2. NO – next stop is the shredder or bin – whichever is closer!

3. MAYBE – the second NO pile, which also usually ends up in the shredder or bin but in the meantime may sit gathering dust on a desk.

Wave two – Taking the YES pile, the executive recruiter or employer reads through each CV in a bit more detail and makes a decision as to whom to invite in for an interview.

Your sole purpose is to make it to wave two and be invited in for the interview.

DIY (Do It Yourself)!

Beware of false prophets; there is only one person who knows you better than anyone else, and that's you. Despite attractive offers in the form of paid-for CV writing services, you and you alone should write your CV.

Don't be tempted to entrust the writing of the most important document you'll write this year to anyone else. It not only will cost you money in terms of a fee but will also likely cost you an interview for the executive position you want.

Start from scratch

Many executive jobseekers treat their CV as an evolving document, which means they update it as time goes on. The result is that their CV becomes longer and longer and, in the process, less and less relevant.

There is another danger lurking; if you simply add to your CV, you may forget what's on it and get caught at the interview on something from the past you'd forgotten was on there.

A number of years ago, I was recruiting a senior finance position for a large international organisation. I'd shortlisted Debbie because she had excellent experience for the position, and my client agreed and invited her in for an interview.

The interview was competency based, and my client asked specific questions to delve into and expand on some really great achievements Debbie had on her CV.

Unfortunately, things didn't go quite according to plan – Debbie couldn't answer some of the questions because she'd written her CV so long ago. She wasn't selected for a second interview, and the process for her stopped there.

Updating a CV in the world of the executive jobseeker is a criminal offence, often punishable by a long and lonely period of failure and frustration.

Compare it to decorating a house and painting over the cracks or existing wallpaper. It might look good on the surface, but sooner or later the cracks will start to show through, and the wallpaper will start to peel.

The only way to write your CV is to start with a blank piece of paper – to start from scratch.

What you will remember is likely to be the most up-to-date, relevant and important information. As you've advanced in your career, much of your earlier experience can be assumed and is superseded by higher-level experience, which should take centre stage.

Write with the reader in mind

Your CV is not about you; it's not about everything you've done in the past or want to do in the future.

It's all about the reader, giving him enough of the right information to make it an easy decision to invite you in for an interview.

While you will have a generic CV (the CV you place on executive job boards and give to recruiters), when applying for a specific executive position, you need to tailor your CV specifically to it.

Most vacancies begin with a job specification, and this is a great starting point to understand what the decision maker is looking for on your CV.

If there are four key skills or types of experience the person is looking for, then these are the specific things you should focus on in constructing your CV.

Where possible, obtain the job specification in advance, and tailor your CV specifically to the position. You can do this whether applying through an executive recruiter or going directly to an employer.

Be warned – a professional recruiter's and employer's favourite game is often SNAP!

Yes, SNAP – the card game that involves matching cards.

For the best chance of landing on the YES pile, mirror the role requirements and reference key words from the job specification that the reader will expect to see.

Remember, as you write your CV (generic or specific), you need to answer the following questions:

1. Who is your target audience (i.e. who is going to read it)?

2. What are they looking for?

Keep it simple

Often the person reading your CV and responsible for the initial filter is not an expert in your field.

If you are a finance director, how likely is it that the executive recruiter or employer vetting your CV will understand all of the technical terms and acronyms relating to the complex world of finance (possibly why they're hiring in the first place)?

He may expect to see certain terms on there that are important in the job specification, but bombarding him with technical jargon in the hope to impress is never a good idea.

If something's too difficult to comprehend, the decision maker may find it easier to bypass you and move on to the next candidate – there are usually plenty to choose from. Professional recruiters and employers are likely to have a number of options – don't overcomplicate. Instead, keep things simple and relevant.

Ever heard the expression 'can't see the wood for the trees'?

Simplicity is also about having the discipline to take away to reinforce the power of what remains.

The temptation is usually the opposite; add as much as possible in the hope that something sticks. Make sure you don't fall into this trap.

Signpost to discuss at the interview

Your CV is not an isolated document. It sets the scene at the outset for the whole recruitment process.

Remember Debbie and how the achievements on her CV were used not only to select her for the interview but also to direct the interview questions?

While the sole purpose of your CV is to get you the interview, it also directs and influences what you'll likely be asked.

Focus on your key achievements – those you are most proud of that highlight you as the best candidate for the position.

Tell great stories with achievements

As children, we all loved stories, and while we won't always admit it, nothing much has changed in adult life.

Nothing changes the dynamic of a boring presentation more than the presenter announcing that he or she is about to tell a story – we're programmed from birth to take notice and pay attention!

Great stories have a start, middle and end. Great achievements on a CV have the same and have much more power than responsibilities.

Responsibilities tell the reader what you do on a day-to-day basis. You might be responsible for managing complex external stakeholder relationships or a large team of people, but there's no story here – there's no reason to sit up and take notice.

Responsibilities are important and should exist on your CV, but they're very much the poor relation to powerful achievements.

Achievements are specific to your ability in a position and go above and beyond what's expected. They're not a day-to-day occurrence, and they supercharge your ability to stand out from the crowd so the reader will take notice.

Let's look at a quick example from my time in the recruitment industry to illustrate the difference between responsibilities and achievements.

Responsibilities:

- *Recruitment of finance directors for SME and large organisations across all industry sectors.*

- *Management and training of a team of 12 consultants.*

(Observations – occurs every day, no story – no 'wow' factor.)

Achievements:

- *Identified an award as an opportunity to raise the profile of the recruitment business (Start). Entered the Chamber of Commerce 'Most Promising New Business' category, which involved completing an application form and being interviewed face to face by the category judge (Middle). Despite strong competition from ten other businesses, won the award, which created numerous PR opportunities and three inbound enquiries converted to £30k worth of fee income* **(End)**.

- *To help jobseekers better understand the job market, wrote a book called* Super Secrets of the Successful Jobseeker *in six months* **(Start)**. *Published by Harriman House in 2013; over 1,500 copies were sold in the first year* **(Middle)**. *The book has received over 50 five-star reviews on Amazon* **(End)**.

(Observations – occurs infrequently, great story with a start, middle and end – has the 'wow' factor.)

Achievements can also be non–work related:

- *In 2006, while living in Japan and looking for a new challenge, enrolled in the International Aikido Senshusei Programme* **(Start)**. *This was an 11-month intensive martial arts boot camp with the Tokyo Riot Police* **(Middle)**. *One of only 150 people in the world to have survived and successfully completed this course* **(End)**.

Get the basics right

Whatever you do, don't forget the basics. You could have the best experience and fantastic achievements packaged together to get you the interview, but get the basics wrong, and all the impact falls away.

Spelling and grammar – There is no excuse for misspelling or bad grammar. Get this wrong, and it tells the recruiter or employer you are sloppy or don't care. Use spellcheck, proofread and then spellcheck and proofread again!

Use third person – Convention dictates that CVs be written in third person. For example: *Responsible for...* and not *I was responsible for...*; the latter can be very annoying.

Structure of a super CV

Before taking a look at a CV template, let's cover a number of all too frequently asked questions (FAQs) on CV content and structure.

CV FAQs

How long should my CV be?

Your CV should be as long as it needs to be – no more, no less. Every sentence should fight for the right to be there. If it doesn't add value, then take it out.

Do I need a cover letter?

If you're asked for one, you must include one – if you don't, you may fall at the first hurdle for failing to follow instructions!

Executive recruiters rarely require a cover letter, but if you are applying directly to an employer, you'll need to include one.

As a general rule, your CV should stand on its own two feet as a complete document that tells the reader she absolutely has to interview you ahead of anyone else.

Should I include a personal summary at the top of my CV?

In my opinion, these are rarely read and lack any real power. They are an unnecessary distraction and, unless specifically requested, should be left out.

For example, *A conscientious and capable individual with excellent communication skills* tells the reader nothing and detracts from the real value in any CV – achievements!

Don't tell the reader of your CV what your key qualities are – let them work these out for themselves from your achievements.

Should I include a photo?

How you look has nothing to do with your ability to do a job unless you're a model. It's a different story on LinkedIn, which we'll cover later on.

I don't have a LinkedIn profile or a blog – what should I do?

You'll need a LinkedIn profile. This is an online and searchable version of all you have to offer. A blog, though not essential, can be very powerful, particularly if it demonstrates a keen interest in the sector in which you're seeking your next opportunity. We'll cover this in more detail later.

What's the point of including hobbies and interests?

Hobbies and interests demonstrate passion, dedication to something and often achievement, all of which are very relevant to success in the work environment.

Having examined many of the common questions, please note the CV template on the next two pages.

THE EXECUTIVE JOBSEEKER CV TEMPLATE

NAME:	Forename | Surname
TELEPHONE:	Home | Mobile
E-MAIL:	yourname@gmail.com
RESIDENCE:	Town or city – willing to relocate?
EDUCATION:	Degree (e.g. BSc, BA (Hons), MSc etc.) – subject – class (e.g. 2.1, 2.2) 'A' levels or equivalent GCSEs / 'O' levels or equivalent
QUALIFICATIONS:	Include pass record / awards
LANGUAGES:	List languages – spoken / written – fluent / intermediate / basic
LINKEDIN:	linkedin.com/in/yourname
BLOG:	yourblog.com

EXPERIENCE

JAN '12–DATE	**Company / Organisation** Brief description of the organisation / industry sector / turnover of group and division.
MAR '13–DATE	**Position**
	Responsibilities: (List key responsibilities)
	Achievements: (List 3 or 4 key achievements)
JAN '12–FEB '13	**Position**
	Responsibilities: (List key responsibilities)
	Achievements: (List 3 or 4 key achievements)
IT SKILLS:	Systems used and to what level?
INTERESTS:	What do you do in your spare time, and to what level?

STEP TWO:

COVER LETTERS

In this section, we'll discuss the cover letter, including its definition, when to use it and how to structure one to deliver maximum impact.

Definition

A cover letter is a letter or e-mail sent along with a CV to support an executive job application or speculative approach, whether directly to an employer or via an intermediary such as a professional recruiter.

Principles

The common mistake most executive jobseekers make with a cover letter is that they duplicate what's already on their CV.

This is a mistake and provides even more text for an executive recruiter or employer to wade through without adding anything new.

A good cover letter exists to support your CV, not duplicate it.

Your CV should be a stand-alone document requiring no introduction that clearly communicates your skills and experience to a recruiter or potential employer.

A cover letter serves to introduce your CV by grabbing the recipient's attention.

When to include

With the advent of modern technology and the ability to upload

CVs to executive job boards and recruitment agency websites, the need to always include a cover letter has been somewhat diminished.

Cover letters do have a place, though, and should be used on two occasions:

1. If you're asked for one. Sometimes an executive recruiter or a potential employer will ask for a cover letter. If they do, you must include one. Not doing so is a simple failure to follow instructions!

2. If you're sending your CV directly to an employer speculatively or for a specific vacancy and there's an opportunity to communicate relevant information to support your candidacy for this position.

Structure

A good cover letter explains why you're contacting the individual and the organisation he works for. It should have impact, introduce the most relevant part of your experience and clarify what happens next.

It does this in three stages – Grabber / Message / Call to Action (CtA).

Take a look at the example below. With my background in recruitment, I'm applying to a fictitious recruitment business called Codex Consultancy. This is a speculative enquiry; the business is not currently advertising any live vacancies.

The letter on the next page is addressed to Mr John Squire, managing director.

Dear John

'Recruitment relies on great PR' – **John Squire**

Many congratulations on your recent win at the London Recruitment Awards. This is a fantastic achievement, and I really enjoyed reading your interview with *Recruiter* magazine afterwards.

I recently led our organisation to win in the 'Most Promising New Business' category at the Chamber of Commerce awards, which created numerous PR opportunities and three inbound enquiries converted to £30k worth of fee income. Like you, I'm a big believer in the power of PR. (Additional information can be found in my attached CV.)

Having followed the success of your business for the past six months, I'm extremely keen to explore opportunities with such a progressive organisation and will give you a call over the next few days to discuss. In the meantime, for contact purposes I can be reached on 07805 567 954 or at simon.gray@careercodex.com.

Yours sincerely

Simon Gray

Let's look at the key elements of this letter in more detail. Note that this could be sent as a hard copy letter in the post, as an attached letter by e-mail or in the body of the e-mail itself.

Grabber – I use John's words from his interview as the subject line and make reference to the recent award in the opening paragraph. This is likely to spark his interest – it's all about him at this stage and has nothing to do with me. I also tell him here that I'm serious enough about him and his business to have read his recent interview.

Message – This links one part of my experience to what's important to John (PR) and supports my CV in inviting him to take a look.

CtA – Again, I tell him how serious I am about his business (I've been following its growth for six months). I keep control of the situation by saying I will call him but give him an option to call or e-mail me in advance. John doesn't need to hunt for my contact details; they're there in the body of the letter.

How different is this approach from that of standard cover letters you may have seen or written yourself in the past?

It is short and well researched, focusing on something important to John. Its initial emphasis is not me looking for a position; it's conversational but makes its point clearly and concisely.

A cover letter such as this has a high probability of maintaining interest and encouraging the reader to take a detailed look at the attached CV.

STEP THREE:

GETTING IN FRONT OF DECISION MAKERS

We have already identified the key players in the executive job market and explored their motivations.

You now know the existence of the hidden market and appreciate why going directly to an employer should be part of any successful executive job search strategy.

In this section, we'll look at how to successfully engage with people who can introduce you or offer you the executive position you've defined in your personal executive jobseeker plan.

Media of approach

Using a balanced portfolio of communication tools provides a better chance of success because much depends on the preferences of the recipient. Some people like e-mail, some prefer social media and others favour the phone.

For example, I'm not a huge fan of e-mail and would much prefer that someone call me directly – I find it more personal, and with my busy schedule, it can be more time efficient.

Combining approaches is an important strategy. In the communication age, we're all bombarded non-stop by information. Sometimes for the most important messages to even get through requires a number of attempts by varying means.

Sending an e-mail and a few days later following up with a phone call and a LinkedIn connection request has a better chance of success than sending e-mail after e-mail, particularly if you're trying to reach me!

Let's look at the pros and cons of some of the most common forms of communication media:

E-mail

Pros

- Quick and efficient.

- Easy to confirm delivery and that your e-mail has been read (read receipt).

- Great communication tool once the initial relationship and associated trust have been established (once you're known, it's more likely your e-mail will be opened).

- Easy to include multiple attachments.

- Ability to send and receive on multiple devices (e.g. phone, tablet and home computer).

Cons

- Favoured by most executive jobseekers, so hard to stand out and easy to get lost in the clutter.

- Requires a good subject line to get noticed – limited space to communicate this message.

- A chance that your e-mail could be rejected as SPAM.

- Easy for the recipient to delete at the click of a button.

- Fear of viruses may mean important attachments remain unopened.

Phone

Pros

- Quick and efficient.

- An effective tool to build a personal relationship in advance of meeting.

Cons

- Often blocked by gatekeepers who are trained not to take your call.

- Easy to miss calls and waste time playing voicemail tennis.

Social Media – e.g. LinkedIn/Twitter

Pros

- Modern and currently a less used and understood form of communication by executive jobseekers.

- Curiosity dictates that on receipt of your message, the recipient is likely to at least view your profile.

- The recipient (depending on user settings) is notified twice – in his inbox and on the social media platform. He has two opportunities to see your message.

- Less prone to SPAM.

Cons

- Limited space to communicate your message (character limits on certain platforms).

- Difficult to include attachments.

- May require the purchase of a premium account (LinkedIn) to contact some people.

Post

Pros

- An often forgotten medium of communication – a letter warrants attention and stands out.

- A handwritten envelope provides additional intrigue and curiosity.

- High chance of getting directly to the decision maker, particularly if marked 'Private and Confidential'.

- Harder to delete than an e-mail and is likely to hang around before being shredded or binned.

Cons

- Not instantaneous delivery.

- No delivery confirmation unless you pay for a premium delivery service.

- Generally takes longer to write than an e-mail or social media message.

Face to Face

Pros

- Results in an instant interview.

- You immediately stand out from the competition.

Cons

- Requires finding the right networking event or the confidence to turn up at a professional recruiter's or employer's premises unannounced.

A word of warning – avoid using all of the above at the same time. Don't e-mail, post a message on LinkedIn and then phone straight away – the recipient might feel she is being ambushed and become less likely to respond.

Make sure you innovate, experiment and, most importantly, have fun. It's just communication and to some extent is trial and error. We all have our particular preferences as to how we like to be reached.

Before we move on from media of approach, let's look at a real-life example that I personally received while running my own recruitment business.

I wasn't even in the market to hire a recruitment consultant, but Matt got my attention from the beginning.

He sent me an introductory e-mail with his CV attached. The subject line caught my eye as it read: *Previous experience in recruitment.* He'd actually done a brief stint working for one of my competitors.

Although this caught my attention, I was busy, got distracted and moved on. Matt's approach, through no fault of his own, made his CV hit the MAYBE pile, and he would require an additional tactic to get through the door.

Matt called me a few days later to confirm I'd received his e-mail. I remembered him and was pleasantly surprised to find an articulate young man on the end of the phone who had clearly researched my business.

I invited him in for a coffee and was very impressed. He came back again the same week for his second interview, and I hired him on the spot!

Matt did three things well:

1. He'd not waited to respond to an advertised vacancy – he made an approach anyway.

2. He was persistent but always polite.

3. He'd researched and was well prepared for our initial phone conversation.

If you've recruited in the past in your business, what would your reaction be if someone approached you in this way? Would the person stand out? Would he get your attention?

Although this was for a relatively junior position, the same lessons apply to the senior executive job market.

While I was working with Rick, a senior executive in the aerospace industry, this topic came up in conversation and went something like this:

Rick – 'I can't really approach senior decision makers directly, can I, when I haven't seen an executive position advertised?'

Me – 'You absolutely can, and the fact that you think this should tell you that the majority of your competition would think this way, too. That's exactly why an approach like this works – you stand out.'

Although there are many ways to approach the decision maker, what really matters is not the medium of approach but the content and positioning of that approach.

The 'executive jobseeker dichotomy'

The 'executive jobseeker dichotomy' is one of the most important principles in the Career Codex methodology and is a framework for all communication between you and the outside world.

A dichotomy is defined as a contrast between two things represented as being opposed or entirely different. In actual fact, the executive jobseeker dichotomy is a double dichotomy and is entirely different from the majority of executive jobseekers' beliefs, thinking and actions.

Let's examine this in detail:

Your success in the executive job market has nothing to do with the executive job market itself; it has everything to do with you.

In all communication with professional recruiters and employers, it's never about you; it's always about them.

Contrast this with how the majority of executive jobseekers think and behave. They think their success in the executive job market depends on current market conditions – things they have no control over. Furthermore, in any engagement with executive recruiters and employers, it's all about the position they want. They feel the need to force their current situation on others at every possible opportunity.

Adopting the executive jobseeker dichotomy as a framework for belief, thinking and action forms the foundation for everything you do to find success in getting in front of the decision maker.

If this sounds a little confusing now, don't worry – all will become clear as we move through the remainder of this section.

Getting in front of the professional recruiter

Recruitment companies and the consultants who work in them are bombarded with e-mails, phone calls and meeting requests day in, day out – and that's just from their candidates.

It's a tough job (I know; I did it for over ten years), and what makes it tougher is that often they're not respected for the job they do.

Let's face it; anyone who has ever written a CV or been in an interview pretty much thinks she gets recruitment. After all, how hard can it be? It's not biophysics, is it? There's a temptation for everyone and anyone to tell the recruiter how to do his job – and nothing annoys him more.

In reality, it is one of the most complicated industries to work in. This is because it involves people on both sides of the transaction – there's an executive jobseeker wanting a job and an employer looking to hire. What adds to this complication is that both are emotional beings with a habit of changing their minds. How they think and react today can be very different from how they are tomorrow. Both take things personally, which affects everything they do, sometimes without them even knowing it.

A professional recruiter has numerous demands placed on her. The candidate wants a job, and the employer wants a candidate. The recruiter is piggy in the middle trying to piece a rapidly moving and emotional puzzle together.

It's the employer (the client) who pays the recruitment fee, and the temptation is to always follow the money!

Naturally, in the pecking order, the professional recruiter gravitates towards the client (rather than towards you, the candidate) and is prepared to invest more time addressing his needs and concerns than yours. If there's a choice between speaking to a new client phoning in with a requirement or a candidate calling to catch up, it doesn't take much effort to figure out whom most recruiters will want to speak to first.

The recruitment industry is notorious for excessive key performance indicator (KPI) driven targets. Executive recruiters feel constantly under pressure to hit numbers and meet targets.

To survive and to protect their own sanity, they've become experts at blocking out information. Under attack from phone calls, e-mails and KPIs, their best defence is often voicemail, out of office or just not getting back to you. This is the reality of their situation, and understanding this helps you, the executive jobseeker, have more productive engagements with them.

For an executive jobseeker, to get through this barrier, it's not about shouting louder; it's about approaching them in a way that is completely different from that of everyone else.

Two key principles underpin successful relationships with executive recruiters.

1. Show them respect

In my very first conversation with Dave, a new executive client who'd approached me for help, I asked him how many recruitment businesses he was registered with. He wasn't sure.

When I pushed him a little more, he guessed at around ten but couldn't be certain.

He was also disparaging and derogatory in how he spoke about the recruitment industry. After all, no one had found him a job yet.

I asked Dave three questions:

1. 'If you don't know whom you're registered with, how can you expect to have a meaningful relationship?'

2. 'If you don't know them, how can you expect them to know you?'

3. 'If you don't respect executive recruiters, how keen do you think they'll be to go the extra mile for you?'

Dave had no answer, but he got the point!

2. Show them you're serious

By registering with multiple recruitment companies, you're basically saying that you don't have much faith in the abilities of any of them to find you the executive position you're looking for. After all, aren't you simply hedging your bets? Professional recruiters are likely to sense this.

Let's bring back Dave and introduce Hannah from ABC Search and Selection. Hannah is likely to have three thoughts about Dave, which are not particularly helpful to him:

1. *How good can Dave really be if he has had to register with so many of my competitors? Furthermore, none of them has managed to place him in an executive position as yet. What's wrong with him?*

2. *If Dave is registered with ten of my competitors, I have a one in ten chance of placing him. I'm probably best to invest my time and energy in someone else!*

3. *I'm not going to tell Dave about any of the executive positions I'm handling. He might tell my competitors, and then I'll have even more competition!*

Even if Dave doesn't disclose to Hannah that he's registered with multiple recruitment businesses, she'll find out. Never try to keep anything from a recruiter – they're extremely resourceful and trained to find out things about you that you didn't even know yourself.

It's better to build an excellent relationship with one or two executive recruiters than to have a poor relationship with many. Where possible, identify who to approach through recommendation and referral while also paying attention to sector specialism and local, national and international reach.

To get in front of the professional recruiter requires a different approach. Doing it will shock them into submission, and they're likely to be very curious and keen to meet you.

Executive recruiters rarely put candidates in front of their clients without meeting them first – it's just too much of a risk.

That's why getting face-to-face time with them is so important. Whatever medium of approach you choose, using the following techniques will make you stand out from your competition and result in a higher probability of your securing a face-to-face meeting with a recruiter.

a) **Acknowledge the recruiters' expertise.** In any initial dialogue with a professional recruiter, explain why you have chosen that organisation.

Think of it as if you were applying directly for a position with that company – specifically what is it about their business that makes them stand out?

For example –

Executive jobseeker:

'I've specifically chosen and am extremely keen to be represented by your organisation in my executive job search.
'From the research I have done on your business, I see that you have an excellent reputation focused on candidate care, and you also represent many of the most prestigious businesses in my specialist sector.'

What the recruiter thinks:

This candidate has really done her research and clearly respects my organisation. I want to help her.
She has picked up on our promise of candidate care. I'd better make sure I look after her!

b) **Offer exclusivity.** As detailed above, many executive jobseekers think that the more recruitment companies they register with, the better chance they have of securing the executive position they want.

While the rationale for this makes sense, in practice it rarely works.

Drawing an interesting parallel with the housing market, if you're selling your house, you usually sign with an estate agent on an exclusive basis (it's usually stipulated in the small print of their contracts and is enforceable at least for an agreed period of time).

Estate agents have upfront costs, including advertising and viewing, that must be incurred to sell your house.

Can you imagine how interested they'd be and the kind of service you'd receive if you told them your house was already on the market with nine of their competitors?

Explaining to a professional recruiter that you've registered with him exclusively (or with him and only one other company) tells him that you're putting your trust in his abilities.

It clearly communicates that you expect something from him – and more importantly, from his perspective, that he has a high probability of placing you.

c) **Show you're committed.** Have a valid and convincing reason for leaving your current position or seeking a new position.

This is where your destination statement comes into full effect. Not only does this help you clarify the executive position you want, but it also enables you to communicate a clear and concise message to those who can help you.

This helps you to stand out from your competition, who in my experience often use unhelpful statements.

Executive jobseeker:

'I'm not in a rush!'
'I'm just seeing what's out there.'
'I'm not going to take the first thing that comes along.'
'I'm just dipping my toe in the market.'

What the recruiter thinks:

This candidate could be wasting my time.

If he can't convince me he's committed, then how will he ever convince my client? It's not worth the risk of putting him forward, regardless of his experience.

What if the first executive job I present to her is the right one? Would she really turn down the opportunity just because it's the first thing she's seen?

He doesn't have a good reason for moving in the executive job market. I could spend loads of time helping him, but when an offer comes through, he'll likely stay put, and I won't get paid!

d) **Ask for their help and advice.** Asking for help isn't a sign of weakness; it's actually a very powerful door opener.

By asking an executive recruiter for help and advice, you are telling her two things:

1. I value your opinion and professional expertise.

2. I will listen to what you tell me and do what you ask me to do.

What the recruiter thinks:

This candidate will take my advice; she's already shown me this by asking for my help.
It's worth my investing time to make her the best she can be because she'll act on this advice.
She's going to make my life much easier and is likely to be very easy to place.

e) **Help them to do their job.** Don't tell a recruiter he needs to work with you because you're good; demonstrate why with great achievements.

Just as the best CVs tell stories in the form of achievements, the best professional recruiters tell powerful stories about their candidates to secure them the interview.

Having powerful achievements on your CV shows an executive recruiter that he needs to meet you; it also shows him how to promote you to his clients.

f) *Explain the long-term relationship.* Good executive recruiters know the importance of long-term relationships.

Candidates they place become clients in time, who then come back and recruit more candidates through them as they advance in their career.

Get this on the table early on, and watch the recruiter pull out all the stops to help you.

Executive jobseeker:

'I understand how the recruitment market works and am really keen to build a long-term relationship with you. I'm very grateful for your help.

'If you help me to secure the executive job I want, I promise to come back to you first whenever I need to recruit moving forward.'

What the recruiter thinks:

If I look after this candidate, I'll make not only one fee but also multiple fees in the future. I need to give this person special attention.

g) *Educate him on your sector.* While executive recruiters are great at recruitment, they're not always experts on the sector they specialise in.

When I was in the recruitment industry, I specialised in placing qualified accountants into senior finance positions. As a qualified accountant myself, I was a rare commodity. I knew the sector inside out whilst many of my colleagues without an accounting background struggled with the terminology, not having a real understanding of what it means to be an accountant.

Offering to help an executive recruiter gain a better understanding of the market he specialises in will often be well received. You help him do his job better, be more successful and make more money.

One way to do this is to send him articles or details of events relating to his industry sector. Executive recruiters are often too busy to see this stuff, and whether it's useful to them or not, it's the thought that counts.

Executive jobseeker:

'If there's anything I can do to help you better understand the sector I work in or the people in it, just let me know.'

What the recruiter thinks:

This candidate wants to help me. In return, I need to help her.

h) **Help them in other ways.** If you're currently working, a good professional recruiter will be looking to replace you once you leave, whether she places you in an executive position herself or not.

Acknowledging this in conversation adds force to her desire to help you – if she places you, she has the potential to double up by backfilling your position, too.

In the recruitment industry, the common term for this is 'good recruitment', and being able to do this consistently not only increases an executive recruiter's earning potential but also boosts her chances of promotion.

Executive jobseeker:

'I appreciate that if you place me in an executive position, you'll be keen to backfill my position. When the time is right, I'll be very happy to introduce you to the right person in the organisation and recommend your services.'

What the recruiter thinks:

This is a candidate I absolutely must place. She's going to push more business my way.

Another way to help is to recommend your friends and colleagues to register with the same recruitment company and to ask them to let the recruiter know that you recommended them.

Finally, having met with an executive recruiter, don't call him to catch up, keep in touch, or find out how things are going.

What's the value in this for him? Think back to the executive jobseeker dichotomy, and always approach with information useful to him. Do this to stand out from your competition, to be the one he remembers and to ensure your position the next time he's compiling a shortlist.

The tactics outlined above are tried and tested. They all serve to build a stronger and mutually beneficial relationship, where the executive recruiter sees the value of helping you ahead of helping other candidates he is also representing.

Getting in front of the employer

In my experience, approaching an employer directly is often one of the things executive jobseekers find most difficult.

Despite having achieved a senior position in an organisation and being used to engaging with stakeholders at all levels, suddenly the conversation is personal.

It's much easier when the employer has already advertised a position on their website or on an executive job board, or has appointed a recruitment business.

However, suggesting to an executive jobseeker that she contact an organisation directly when no position is being advertised, often leads to her making excuses, justifications and assumptions as to why this is probably not such a good idea.

I'll probably be wasting my time – **an excuse**. You don't know that, and you're already wasting precious time by deliberating whether to do this or not.

I don't want to intrude or bother them – **a justification**. Who says you'll be bothering them? What if they are at the early stages of making a decision to hire, and you're the perfect candidate?

There's no point; they're not recruiting – **an assumption**. Businesses are always recruiting if the right candidate knocks on the door. Astute organisations know that waiting to hire until they need to hire doesn't guarantee that the right candidate will be available and on the market. They know that often the best time to hire is when the candidate appears and is available!

Think back to the executive job market environment and the three conversations employers have when they need to recruit. They often find the recruitment process painful, distracting and costly in terms of time and fees paid to executive job boards or recruitment companies. If you happen to approach their business in the right way and at the right time, you have the potential to save them time and money.

You now understand the hidden market in which a high proportion of executive positions are filled before ever being advertised or fronted by recruiters. In the hidden market, often your only competition for an executive position yet to be advertised or created to take advantage of your skills and experience is you. No one else is in the process – it's simply you against you, which offers an extremely high probability of success!

By approaching an organisation directly, you're not wasting your time, you're not bothering them, and they might just be recruiting without having gone to market. This is the best time for you to knock on the door.

Through the work you did on planning, the creation of your destination statement and with a little research, you have a target audience to approach regardless of whether or not they are currently recruiting.

Many of the principles and techniques of securing a face-to-face meeting with a professional recruiter are the same when approaching an employer directly.

Remember the second part of the executive jobseeker

dichotomy – in engaging with executive recruiters and employers, it's always about them and never about you.

Taking this a stage further – in approaching the hidden market, it's never about finding an executive job. Instead it's about showing a genuine interest in an organisation through extensive research and enquiring as to whether there is an opportunity for you to help or contribute in some way.

How to find the decision maker

It's sometimes hard to identify an organisation's decision maker from the outside looking in.

Generally, a great place to start is with the people at the top of an organisation – such as the owner, managing director, CEO or similar, who have the most decision-making power.

Such a person is often the spokesperson for his business, so he may have been quoted in the press or on the news section of their website. Cross reference this to LinkedIn, which I'll cover later in this book, to make sure you have his current position correct because news items go out of date, but social media profiles are usually kept up to date.

Information normally flows from the top down in any organisation. This is why it's always best to start at the top, where the future of the organisation is planned and the bigger picture is seen.

If your skills and experience catch the attention of the person at the top of the business, even if she is not the ultimate decision maker, she is very likely to point you in the right direction.

'Marketmakers'

In an earlier chapter, we identified the key players in the executive job market, namely employers and executive jobseekers.

In addition, there are executive job boards and professional recruiters who also play a role.

'Marketmakers' as I've badged them are the fifth player in the executive job market. They're harder to spot because they tend to exist in the hidden market, but they have immense power through their connections and networks.

Marketmakers are influential figures within an industry sector; they're well known and respected, and they possess an enviable contact book.

You could spend time contacting 100 organisations individually, but imagine if you built a relationship with the chief executive of a networking organisation that has those 100 businesses in its membership.

Developing a relationship with this one individual would give you access to potentially all of these organisations in one hit. What's more, an introduction from an influential marketmaker has increased power; it comes with an implicit recommendation.

Marketmakers are easy to find if you know where to look. They're often quoted in the press or industry magazines, and they turn up as guest speakers at business events.

Your competition – other executive jobseekers – won't know of their existence, and even if they did, they may lack the confidence or skills to approach them.

The great news is that marketmakers thrive on making new connections, and providing that you approach in a professional manner and within the framework of the executive jobseeker dichotomy, you're likely to receive a positive response.

Acknowledging their influence and success, followed by asking for help and advice, is a great way to open new doors through their extensive and powerful connections.

Clive, whom I introduced at the start of this book, had an interest in Thomas Cook, one of the world's leading leisure travel groups. At the time, Harriet Green OBE was the CEO.

We found her on Twitter, and through this medium, we gained an insight into her interests away from the office. Then through a cover letter with an attached CV (just as I showed you earlier), Clive made an approach.

Harriet received Clive's correspondence and spoke behind the scenes with the HR team at Thomas Cook, who contacted Clive directly to arrange an interview.

There are three important points to notice here:

1. Thomas Cook wasn't advertising a senior executive position at the time.

2. Clive's approach was positioned following the executive jobseeker dichotomy principle.

3. Approaching the most senior person in the organisation resulted in an implicit recommendation to HR.

Combined, these factors resulted in a face-to-face meeting, which is a precursor to an executive position either now or in the future.

Clive had the meeting, and despite there being nothing quite suitable at that exact moment, he put himself in pole position for any future executive opportunities with an organisation he'd actively targeted in a proactive and innovative way.

STEP FOUR:

THE FIRST-CLASS EXECUTIVE INTERVIEW

Most executive jobseekers approach the interview stage of the recruitment process from a completely wrong angle.

They see an interview as an interrogation, a scenario in which a prospective employer will try to catch them out by asking them impossible questions that they'll undoubtedly struggle to answer.

To prepare, they do what their competitors (other executive jobseekers) do and rote learn a series of standard answers to anticipated questions.

They're on the back foot from the very beginning and approach the interview with fear and dread – not the best starting point for a successful outcome!

Before we look at the interview process in detail, let's dispel some of the myths.

Dispelling the myths

They asked you. Unless you put a gun to their head, it's highly likely that the employer requested to meet you. Out of all the other candidates they could have seen, they chose you. This means they've seen something in your application that sparked their interest – something stood out!

You're there because there is a serious possibility that they will hire you – you've earned your right to be there.

No one is trying to catch you out. The majority of interviewers want the interview to go well. There will always be exceptions to this rule, but I'd question why you'd want to work for an organisation that would deliberately try to catch you out in the first place.

Think about it – why would an employer waste their valuable time meeting you only to make you fail?

Employers don't want to find themselves in an uncomfortable situation in which the dialogue is stilted and the conversation isn't flowing any more than you do.

They're probably under pressure from their superiors to hire quickly and want to get things done efficiently so that they can get back to their day job. The interviewer is your ally – you're meeting him because the organisation wanted you there in the first place.

The interviewer needs your help. Unless she's an experienced HR professional, you're likely to be interviewed by someone just as nervous as you are.

Unless the business you're meeting with recruits on a regular basis, it's likely that the people you come face to face with are fairly inexperienced interviewers.

Employers find the recruitment process an unwanted distraction and are therefore unlikely to distract their senior team further by putting them through a formal interview training process.

In addition, as we've already discussed, most people think they understand how the job market works because at some point in their career, they've had a job.

This reinforces the belief that just because they've been in an interview, they're automatically competent interviewers. Nothing could be further from the truth.

Interviewing is a hard job – a very hard job! It's particularly tough and tiring when done back to back. The employer needs every bit of help you can give him.

It's your decision, too. An interview is not just a meeting in which an employer decides on your suitability for her company and position; it's also one in which you decide if the organisation and opportunity are right for you.

Just as the employer has the right to reject you after the interview, you have the same right to thank them for their time and move on.

It's two-way traffic. An interview is not about you, the executive jobseeker, deflecting a barrage of questions; it's a two-way conversation.

You have the opportunity to make statements and ask questions that guide the conversation to focus on the things that are important – the things that will help the interviewer make the right decision to hire you.

We'll explore these further as we move through this section, but for the moment, remember the following:

An interview is simply a meeting.

It's a meeting of at least two individuals who are looking to identify common ground with each other and to establish whether they can work together.

The two keys to success

There are two inextricably linked keys to success in any interview process.

They are *confidence* and *preparation*.

Through the preparation process, confidence is built, and growing confidence encourages more in-depth preparation – one reinforces the other.

Let's look at both in greater detail.

Confidence

You may have received the all-too-common advice to imagine the interviewer naked.

We've probably all heard this and at some point may have even tried it. I can tell you it rarely works!

It doesn't work because it has no foundation, no substance and no place in an executive jobseeker's arsenal of tools and techniques for success.

Confidence is about being able to perform under pressure. It's about taking the initiative and controlling the interview process from start to finish, regardless of what the employer does or doesn't ask you.

Preparation

In the recruitment industry, there's a well-known saying:

'The best prepared candidate gets the job.'

In my experience, this is true.

Notice that it's not necessarily the best candidate but instead the best prepared one. This is a hugely important distinction.

Think about it; the people you're up against in any interview process are likely to have a background similar to yours.

Through preparation, you have the opportunity to stack the odds in your favour because preparation gives you confidence. Knowing more about the organisation and person you are meeting, you have the ability to have a higher-level conversation from the start.

Preparation requires time, so accepting an interview with only an hour's notice is never a good idea. Give yourself the time you'll need to prepare, to position yourself as the one to impress.

Just as a professional boxer trains hard to fight easy, you, too, must prepare hard to ensure the best interview possible.

The staircase of preparation

Preparation is like a staircase in a big old house with rooms coming off each landing.

As you climb, you discover more about the old property and must explore each room properly before ascending to the next level.

Most executive jobseekers never make it past the basement. They look at the company's website, and that's it.

Remember, to find success in the executive job market, you have to stand out from the crowd. Simply copying what other executive jobseekers are doing as a blueprint for success is a one-way ticket to failure.

As you climb, there are things you need to research at both the organisation and individual level.

For the purposes of this section, I've assumed only one interviewer. For multiple interviewers, it's the same process but more work.

Let's take a detailed look at each level in turn.

Basement

Organisation

Website – Most executive jobseekers focus solely on the About Us page, but you should dig deeper and look at the organisation's Products or Services pages to understand what they're selling and to whom.

The News page normally contains a wealth of information on what the business is currently doing or planning to do. Usually what's on this page is information the company is extremely proud of and will be keen to talk about, which makes it a great icebreaker or interview question.

Social media – What do the company's LinkedIn page, Twitter feed or other social media profiles say about it? Look for additional insights that aren't on the website. In many organisations, social media is instantaneous, whereas the website can and often does take much longer to update.

Individual

CV – Know your CV inside out. It's usually critical to your getting the interview in the first place. What does it say about you, and how does it relate to the job specification for the position?

If you have the opportunity to do so before the interview, ask the employer what caught their eye and prompted them to ask to meet you. It's a good clue as to what's important and what they're likely to focus on at the interview.

A useful technique is to take a piece of paper and draw a line down the middle.

Read the job specification three times, and place it face down.
On the left-hand side of the paper, write down the four or five things that are critical to the role as identified in the job specification, as you see them.

Next read your CV three times and place it face down.

Now on the right-hand side, write down examples in the form of achievements that directly relate to the left column. This is the experience you must communicate at the interview.

First floor

At basement level, you've done the bare minimum that any executive jobseeker must do ahead of any interview. Now as we advance to the first floor, the preparation work you do begins to make you really stand out from the competition.

Organisation

Internet search – A Google search on the business can reveal lots of information that you may not find on the website (both good and sometimes not so good).

It gives you an accurate picture of not only what the company says about itself through its website and social media channels but also what others may be saying, with or without the company's knowledge.

Furthermore, it's the source for the very latest news. Imagine that the organisation you're meeting has won an important contract on the day of your interview. Don't you think you should know about it and that the employer would expect you to acknowledge the company's success?

Company information – In the UK, you can look up information on an organisation's ownership and finances at Companies House (companieshouse.gov.uk). If you're not based in the UK, there will be a similar website in your country.

This gives you more of a historical perspective of the company but also provides a useful comparison to current performance and market conditions.

For a nominal fee, you can download the latest accounts and

other company information.

Company literature – What does the company you are meeting with send out to its customers, and more importantly, have you read this information?

You should phone reception or the organisation's marketing department and ask them to post out some publicity material to you.

They may refer you to the website as a source of information, but be firm and request hard-copy information in the post. It's important and has another use on the day of the interview, which we'll cover later.

Individual

LinkedIn – Make sure you've looked at the LinkedIn profile of the person you are meeting.

- What's his background, and where has he worked in the past?
- Where was he educated, and did you attend the same school or university?
- What does he do outside of work, and what are his hobbies and interests?
- What is he posting in his status updates? What does this tell you about his current thinking and what's important to him?

Viewing their profile tells the employer in advance of the interview that you're preparing properly – LinkedIn will alert them to the fact.

In turn, they may look back at you, which makes it extremely important that your profile tells the right story – more on this later.

It's too early for you to send a connection request. Save this as part of your post-interview follow-up strategy.

Second floor

Organisation

Market information – Knowing something about the industry that the business you're meeting operates in gives you excellent background information. It's knowledge you can leverage at the interview in the form of intelligent comments or insightful questioning and will further help you stand out from your competition.

There is a lot of free information on the Internet that gives an overview of a particular market sector on what's happening and what's important.

Google is a great starting point, as is Key Note (keynote.co.uk), or similar, which offers paid industry reports with a free executive summary.

Individual

Contacts in common – Whom do you know in common? LinkedIn is a great tool to find this out, as you can easily identify connections you have in common.

It's an opportunity for you to speak to a mutual connection you know reasonably well ahead of the interview to get useful background information on the person you'll be meeting.

It can also be a great icebreaker:

'I understand you used to work with Mary from XYZ Limited.'

Be careful, though; you must speak to the mutual connection in advance to fully understand the relationship.

It must be someone who will speak favourably about you and also someone with whom the interviewer has a good relationship and will recognise by name.

A connection on LinkedIn doesn't always guarantee a personal or favourable relationship, so it's best to check this out beforehand.

It's worth investing the time to do this – how powerful to be able to talk to someone who knows the person you're meeting ahead of time to gain an insight into her personality and what makes her tick.

A contact that you both know and trust gives both sides credibility and confidence at the outset. It can also put you ahead of your competition. They may not have a common relationship or, worse, still may not have identified it and therefore not leveraged it!

Third floor

Organisation

Experience the organisation – Think about the organisation you are meeting with. Do they have outlets or a product that you can experience?

You might be meeting the owner of a retail organisation. How powerful would it be to visit one or more of the stores, chat with the manager on-site about what's happening in the business and perhaps even gain an insight into the person you will be meeting?

Innovative thinking like this really sets you apart from your competition.

The fact that you've made the effort is often more important than any information gained. It tells the person you are meeting a lot about your interest in his organisation.

Get the name of the person you meet and give him yours – the interviewer may hear of the meeting ahead of your interview.

It all starts with walking into the store and starting a conversation.

'Excuse me; I wonder if you can help me please. I have an interview at Head Office next week (mention by name the person who is interviewing you) and was hoping to have a quick chat with the manager to understand a bit more about the business, please.'

There might not be a shop front, but there can be other ways to experience an organisation – it just requires some thinking.

For many years, I recruited for a regional airline and encouraged my candidates to experience the product.

Now, the ideal way to do this would be to take a flight, but given the cost consideration and time available, this was not always possible.

Instead, what was possible – and also more cost effective – was to get online and experience the flight-booking process first-hand (the booking could easily be aborted prior to checkout).

Was the booking process easy? What else did it tell you, and what feedback on your customer experience could you give the person you're meeting?

Customers and suppliers – Successful businesses are not islands; they have customers and suppliers. Researching an organisation's key customers and suppliers takes your knowledge of the organisation to a whole new level.

Individual

Know the summary – As you'll discover shortly, thorough research is the key to controlling any interview, but it requires that you have a clear picture of all you have done and what it means.

Just as you need knowledge of your CV, which is a summary of your skills, experience and, most importantly, achievements relevant to the position, you must have a summary of the research you have done and what it tells you about the organisation and individual you are meeting.

This clear summary is what you need to know and must communicate at the outset of any interview to stand out from your competition.

Having come this far, there's one more level to ascend. It's a level closed to most executive jobseekers – they've either stopped climbing already or are still in the basement.

It's the roof terrace, and it's the level that gives you the opportunity to really wow the employer either during or after the interview.

Roof terrace

90-day plan – As a professional recruiter, I lost count of how many times I heard one of my clients utter the following words as part of his position and person-specification brief:

'I want this person to hit the ground running!'

Having invested time in the recruitment process, not to mention the starting salary and benefits package, employers are ideally seeking an immediate return on their investment.

Sometimes this isn't practical because there is a training requirement or an induction process to go through. However, it's not about what's practical or not; it's about the lengths you have gone to impress and subsequently stand out from your competition.

A 90-day plan is the culmination of all the research you have done and tells an employer in a brief summary document what you would do, if hired, in your first three months with the organisation.

Your caveat is that it's based on the research you have been able to do (itemise the research you have done at the start of the plan) from the outside looking in. There are things you can never know before your feet are firmly under the table.

It's preparation in case the employer asks you a question on what you would do having started with the business, or it's something to leave behind at the end.

I've personally used this strategy to great effect.

In my interview for a part-time chief executive position running a business-networking organisation with a focus on driving inward investment, I was up against two candidates with far more experience in the sector.

This was stiff competition; I'd never run a business-networking organisation before and knew very little about inward investment.

I knew this and understood that to secure the position, I would need to go the extra mile.

I did all of the research and created a 90-day plan.

At the interview, I mentioned my 90-day plan and offered to talk through what I'd put together.

I didn't force my plan upon them but instead gave them the opportunity to ask me to run through it – this is an important distinction.

The four interviewers (yes, there were four of them) agreed, and the whole focus of the interview changed from a review of my CV and experience (what I'd done in the past) to what I would actually do in the future.

Because I had this conversation with the panel, they were already visualising me in the role taking action and getting things done.

Their standard questions went out the window, and I was now firmly in control of the interview process.

Despite the other two candidates having more experience, they offered me the job!

We've now covered how to properly prepare for any interview, which involves researching the organisation, the individuals you'll meet and yourself. This takes time and should never be left to the last minute.

Let's now move to the day of the interview, when everything you've done so far comes together.

The day of the interview

Dress appropriately – This usually means business attire and polished shoes. Don't leave this to the last minute and decide on what you're wearing the night before.

Leave with plenty of time – You can never predict traffic, so make sure you leave with time to spare.

Being late, whatever the reason, is bad manners and should be avoided at all costs.

If you're unsure of the location, it's a good idea to do a test run a few days before and, if possible, at the time you'll be travelling.

Your interview starts from the moment you arrive on-site. If you're driving, it's the moment you pull into the car park.

Buildings usually have windows, and as you approach where your interview will take place, you are highly visible – people just might be watching!

Make sure you acknowledge everyone you meet, which includes speaking to the receptionist while you wait for the interviewer to arrive. This has power for two reasons:

1. It's a last opportunity to find out what the person you're meeting is like, what makes her tick and anything else that could prove useful.

2. The interviewer may ask the receptionist for his opinion. When I interviewed staff for my own recruitment business, I used to do this all the time. People can behave differently with different people, and as an interview is something of an artificial environment, I wanted to see what any prospective employee was really like.

Controlling the interview

Remember the myths we discussed? Remember the first part of the executive jobseeker dichotomy? Your success or failure at the interview is totally dependent on you.

You have done extensive research and are empowered to unleash the skills and techniques to control the interview from start to finish, regardless of what the interviewer asks or fails to ask.

Let's now take a detailed look at the ways you can take control and run the interview process according to your agenda from the very start.

Start strong

Standing room only – Never sit in the reception; always stand. The seats may look comfy and you might be invited to sit, but it's best avoided as doing so puts you at a psychological disadvantage from the start.

In traditional Far Eastern cultures, the more elevated someone is, the more important he is. Don't put the employer in this powerful position from the beginning by having to rise from your chair.

Sitting down can also make you too relaxed, and rising from a seat and gathering your bits and pieces can feel and look awkward.

Stay standing, alert, calm and ready to greet your interviewer with good eye contact and a firm handshake.

Break the ice – Remember the company literature you obtained as part of your preparation? This is the time to be carrying it, as it visually shows the interviewer that you've taken the trouble to obtain it and that you already know something about her organisation.

Now is the time to reference something you've gleaned from your research in the form of a question.

For example:

'Many congratulations – I read in the news this morning that you've just won a new contract. How's this likely to impact the business?'

Or:

'I was speaking to Jenny Jones the other day (a common connection on LinkedIn), whom I understand you know? She sends her best wishes!'

These icebreakers have much more power than discussing the weather or your journey in. Use your research to be creative, interesting and different!

Establish a higher baseline

As already discussed, it's common for executive jobseekers to be interviewed by inexperienced interviewers. They're often poorly prepared and nervous themselves, which means they can start to talk and never stop.

If the interview is scheduled for an hour, they may talk for at least half of this time – at you and not with you about their organisation.

Having researched, you should know most of this already, and while it is all very interesting, this situation gives you very little opportunity to demonstrate your skills, experience and expertise.

Numerous candidates I've met over the years told me in giving feedback from their interview that the interviewer just talked and talked at them. Don't let this happen to you!

Be first – In the world of martial arts, there's a saying: *'Be first'.* This means getting your attack in first to throw your opponent off guard and put him immediately on the back foot.

Striking first in a combat situation gives you a great opportunity to control things from the start, which often dictates the future direction of the fight.

Having arrived in the interview room, starting the conversation with a statement similar to the following takes the initiative and puts you firmly in the driving seat.

'Thank you for inviting me in for an interview today. Just to let you know before we start, I've done extensive research on your business, including reading your company brochure, visiting a store (or similar, depending on how you've experienced the organisation) and preparing a 90-day business plan.'

It's important to make the distinction between telling the interviewer what you've done to research and bombarding him with everything you know. Remember, it's his business, so he knows what you know – you don't need to tell him.

Explaining to him that you're well prepared, however, enables the interviewer to elevate the level of conversation – it establishes a higher baseline.

Let's use a quick example using two scenarios to illustrate this point.

In my spare time, I trade foreign currency. It's a fairly complicated business with a steep learning curve and is not well understood by the majority of people I meet.

Scenario one:

I bump into Jane at the gym, and in conversation, she asks me what I do in my spare time. I tell her that I trade foreign currency. Assuming she's unlikely to know anything about it, I begin to explain at a very basic level what it's all about.

Scenario two:

Imagine, though, if Jane is also a foreign currency trader. If I had known this at the outset (because she'd stopped me and told me), we could have had a far more productive, interesting and thought-provoking conversation.

In scenario one, I talked too much and bored Jane with things she already knew. I talked while she listened, and it's likely she'll avoid me the next time she sees me. In scenario two, we have an interesting and high-level conversation. We arrange to get together again.

A real-life example:

A meeting with a new client is much the same as an interview in the world of recruitment.

While running my own recruitment business, I often had to travel to meet prospective new clients and pitch for their business.

In a people business, I knew they would judge my performance at the meeting and that this would be a major factor in whom they ultimately decided to hire.

Turning up and giving the same presentation as my competitors might win me the business, but it would never be a high-probability strategy.

To succeed, I had to wow the prospective client, control the meeting and give them no alternative but to appoint me as their chosen recruiter.

One such meeting springs to mind and draws on many of the principles in this book.

I was introduced by a marketmaker contact to a London-based business that, due to continued growth, now needed to recruit a full-time finance director. As my firm was based in the East Midlands, I knew that winning this business against local London recruitment specialists would be tough. My preliminary research told me that the company was in the toy business and owned a number of well-known brands popular with young children.

A few days before my meeting, I visited the Nottingham branch of Toys 'R' Us to search out their product.

I watched as customers passed the display to see how they interacted with the toys. I took photos of the stand and also purchased a number of toys to take home to my children – again, this would be another opportunity to watch the end customer interact with the product.

I spoke with the store manager of the branch to find out how popular the products were with customers and made a note of his name. This was just part of my research for the meeting but was possibly the most important thing I did to prepare.

Arriving in London at the office of my prospective client, I felt prepared and confident. I knew I had gone the extra mile to secure the business and that it was highly likely I had done far more in terms of preparation than any of my competitors who would also be pitching for the opportunity.

In my experience, many recruiters default to selling mode. They try to demonstrate their ability by talking about themselves – how long they've been in business, their impressive client base and how competitive their rates are.

The problem with this approach is that the prospective client has heard it all before. Faced with this, the client's decision is often based on price, as there's really nothing else to set one apart from the others.

I knew that to stand out, I would need to be bold, brave and innovative in my approach.

Here's what happened:

Me: 'Thank you very much for inviting me down to London today to understand more about your business and how I can potentially help.

'I'm really impressed with your product, as are my children. I was actually looking at one of your displays in Toys 'R' Us in Nottingham a few days ago.'

Client: 'Were you? I didn't realise we had any of our product stocked in Nottingham.'

Me: 'Yes, you do. Martin, the store manager, explained to me it was one of the most popular displays in the whole store. Would you like to see a photo?'

Client: 'Yes, for sure!'

(I reach into my bag and pull out a photograph of the display and also the toys I had purchased for my children.)

The rest, as they say, is history!

In the space of a few minutes, I'd convinced them I was the person they needed to hire to find their finance director. I'd gone the extra mile to establish a higher baseline from the start and made the conversation all about them and not about me.

They agreed to my standard fee and to pay a proportion of it upfront as a retainer – there was no negotiation on price.

Create a conversation

A conversation occurs when there's back and forth. One person speaks while the other listens, and then the direction reverses.

Asking questions creates conversations – a question by its very design invites the other party to speak and join the discussion.

In an interview, there's always a risk of being hit with a barrage of questions.

Interviewer – *asks a question.*

Candidate – *answers the question and waits for the next one.*

Interviewer – *asks another question.*

Candidate – *answers this second question and waits for the third.*

In the above exchange, how much control does the candidate have?

The answer is very little indeed.

What if the interviewer fails to ask the right questions that might enable the candidate to demonstrate she's the right person for the job?

The candidate could be rejected from the process despite having all of the skills, experience and more – what a wasted opportunity!

As an executive jobseeker, you can and should ask questions during your interview; they're not just reserved for the end.

Asking questions disrupts the interviewer's ability to interrogate and dissolves his power.

Let's look at the above example again, but this time the candidate changes the dynamic:

Interviewer – *asks a question.*

Candidate – *answers the question and asks the interviewer a related question.*

Interviewer – *answers the question and asks her second question.*

Candidate – *answers this second question and asks for further confirmation or clarification on an area related to the topic.*

The black hole principle

Nobody likes an awkward silence, and as human beings, we go out of our way to avoid them.

They are, however, a very powerful tool in your arsenal to control any interview situation. In addition, they're an opportunity to emphasise a point or to switch roles from speaker to listener, important in any conversation.

Let's make a couple of observations:

1. Powerful communicators speak slowly and with confidence, and they use the power of the pause. They pause to emphasise the point and drive their message home, which also gives the listener the opportunity to digest what's being said before returning with their own comment.

2. On a CV, large paragraphs of text are not appealing to the eye. Instead, bullet points and intermittent white space encourage the reader to continue.

Don't be afraid of silence; use it to your advantage to emphasise your point or to change roles in the conversation.

A good interviewer uses this principle to his advantage. By creating a black hole, he lures the candidate in. The natural tendency is to fill the gap. If not careful, the candidate begins to waffle, speed up and lose composure.

I often used this technique when interviewing senior candidates. It was a way to test their communication skills and also to extract additional information they perhaps hadn't planned to tell me.

The *8 Mile* strategy

8 Mile is an American hip-hop biopic film starring Eminem, who plays a young white rapper named Jimmy 'B-Rabbit' Smith Jr.

B-Rabbit's fortunes are determined by his ability to battle, which involves trading insults on stage (communicated through rap) with a willing opponent.

In one of the final scenes of the film, B-Rabbit faces his nemesis in the form of Papa Doc, the leader of the Free World gang and an infamous battler.

B-Rabbit knows what he's up against. Undeterred, he goes first and turns his insults on himself, acknowledging his poor upbringing and *white trash* roots.

Having pre-empted Papa Doc's attack, the infamous battler is left with no rebuttal and no power – he hands the microphone back to the MC and bows his head in defeat.

So what does this have to do with the executive job market and, more specifically, an interview situation?

Well, we all have things in our past and on our CV that we'd prefer to hide.

There might be gaps in our experience or something else that if left unacknowledged could have a negative impact on our being offered the position.

Let's look at a fictional example to demonstrate how to use the *8 Mile* strategy to your advantage.

Jacky is on her second interview with MaxiSam Ltd and meeting John Cripwell, the CEO, in what she understands to be her last and final interview before a decision is made.

Her first interview was with Charles Booth, the human resources director, and it took place three weeks ago – plenty of time for both parties to forget what had happened and what was said.

Jacky has been diligent. Straight after her first interview, she wrote notes on what was discussed and, more importantly, what seemed to go well and what went less well. She documented this while it was fresh in her mind and before the passage of time had the power to distort reality.

Ahead of and as part of her preparation for her second interview, Jacky digs out these notes. She doesn't just read them to refresh her memory; she interrogates them, on the lookout for clues.

Jacky knows that it's highly likely that Charles will brief John ahead of her second interview, but even if he doesn't, John (working for the same organisation) may reach similar conclusions.

Back in her notes, Jacky finds that she was pressed by Charles on her decision to relocate from London to Scotland, where the position is based. She also notes that the conversation focused intensely for a time on her lack of experience in the engineering sector (MaxiSam Ltd is a precision engineering company).

There were also points where Charles appeared impressed and very reassured by her competence. This included her knowledge of international markets.

We have a natural tendency to hide our weaknesses, to brush them under the carpet and hope they go away. The problem is that they rarely disappear, and even if John fails to explore Charles' reservations at the second interview, there's a strong possibility of these being factored into his decision.

Jacky uses the *8 Mile* strategy to her advantage as follows –

Reservation one:

'Charles, I understand that you may have a reservation surrounding my relocation from London to Scotland. I wanted to reassure you that I am actively looking to buy a property in the Paisley area and am registered with three estate agents. In the short term, I am happy to rent and have already viewed two properties that are suitable and immediately available.'

(Notice that because she is specific, her explanation carries more power. She mentions Paisley, three estate agents and that she has found two suitable rental properties.)

Reservation two:

'I appreciate that you may have a concern over my lack of specific experience in the engineering sector. My background in manufacturing is closely related, and I've moved sector twice before with no issue. If anything, being able to provide fresh insights enabled me to add more value from day one.'

She then goes on to provide a specific example in story form – with a start, middle and end.

If John (like Papa Doc) had a microphone, he'd have probably put it down by now.

Using the *8 Mile* strategy, Jacky has addressed John's likely concerns (and Charles', too) and left nothing to perception, assumption or chance.

Fill in the gaps

Towards the end of the interview, having given the interviewer plenty of opportunity to ask you first, you have to fill in any gaps.

Remember, interviewers are not always experienced and sometimes lack the ability to ask the right questions to draw out your best and most relevant experience.

As you are controlling the interview, leaving without having played your best cards is unacceptable.

From your research, you should have a good idea as to what the employer's key decision factors (the things they need as evidence to make the decision to hire) are and your experience in these areas.

If you've not been asked a question that allows you to demonstrate your experience against these decision factors, don't leave things to chance – volunteer this information.

Let's bring Jacky back in:

'John, I know from my research that MaxiSam Ltd operates in multiple international markets. I have had significant experience while at Scotshin Ltd working in China, India and Russia. We've not covered this in our conversation, but I would be more than happy to discuss it if this is of interest.'

Jacky knows that her international experience will help her application. John may not be prepared or could have forgotten to cover this, and Jacky gives him an easy way to get back on track. Notice, too, that she doesn't force her experience on him; she offers to share, which is very different.

Knowledge-based questions

An unwritten rule states that to progress to the next stage of the recruitment process, you must ask questions at the end of your interview.

Questions show you're interested, they show you've been listening, and they're a great way to end the interview on the higher baseline, which you established at the start.

Questions are also an opportunity for you to be creative and to differentiate yourself from other candidates. This is especially the case when interviewers interview from a standard script or a list of standard questions.

Questions are one of the most powerful ways to control the interview and leave a lasting impression on those you meet.

First of all, let's look at a couple of key principles:

1. You must ask questions even if you're not prompted to do so – but you must ask permission to ask them.

2. Never ask anything you could find out for yourself – it's a wasted question, and you will have missed the opportunity to elevate things to a higher level.

(It should go without saying that you never ask questions about salary, holidays or hours of work. These are not knowledge-based questions and should be reserved for when they become relevant – once you've been offered the position.)

Let's look at how Jacky handles the situation when she's not prompted to ask questions:

'John, just before we finish, I have a few questions – do you have a few moments for me to ask them now, please?'

Knowledge-based questions come in two forms – ***belters*** and ***builders***.

Belters introduce original content not yet discussed at interview. They're belters because they're exceptional and are designed to wow and impress the interviewer.

'From my research, I understand that one of your competitors has recently opened operations in Tokyo, Japan. What impact is this likely to have on your business, and how do you plan to respond?'

(The competitor has not been previously mentioned in the interview. This is a challenging question and shows that Jacky has researched not only the organisation but also their competitors.)

Builders build on topics discussed during the interview process. They show that you've been listening and can sometimes be a get-out-of-jail card if your mind goes blank and you can't think of anything to ask.

'You mentioned at the start of our discussion today that you are relatively new in the post. I'm very keen to understand your vision for the business and how you would see me supporting it.'

(This builds on something mentioned earlier. Giving someone the opportunity to talk about him or herself is also a great idea – as human beings, we seem naturally programmed to do this. Furthermore, in the way this question is phrased, Jacky is saying to the interviewer, 'You're important, and I can and want to help you.')

Plan the topics you want to ask questions on before your interview, but never prepare them in advance.

Rote-learned questions sound rehearsed and can break the natural flow of the interview. There's also a danger that you may ask a question on something already covered, which makes you look like you've not been listening.

Remember, an interview should be a conversation and not a barrage of one-way questions. Make sure you converse throughout the interview, but always be prepared to ask your knowledge-based belters and builders at the end – it's expected!

Tell them what you think, and ask for feedback

At the end of the interview, why leave things in limbo? It's far more useful to depart knowing what the interviewer thinks of you and to also give your feedback.

It's always best to maintain control and let interviewers know what you think first, as it can often influence their final impression of you.

It's not time to bury your head in the sand; there's also a final opportunity to deal with any reservations before you leave.

Let's get back to Jacky:

'Just before I leave today, I wanted to let you know how very interested I am in this position. This is a very exciting organisation and one where I know I can make a great contribution.'

By communicating this, Jacky leaves the interview on an extremely positive note.

The interviewer also knows that if he offers Jacky the position (subject to the right remuneration package being negotiated), she is very likely to accept, or if there is to be a next interview stage, she is almost certain to come back.

Now Jacky asks the interviewer for his opinion. She does this because it's an opportunity to gain instant feedback and also to deal with any final reservations should they come up.

'I appreciate that it might be too soon, but do you have any feedback for me at this stage or any comments regarding my suitability for the position, please?'

Remember, this is just feedback, and as she's asked for it, she needs to take it on the chin; whatever the interviewer says at this point, Jacky greets it with a smile and a thank you.

There's a fine line between arguing back against feedback (not a good idea) and dealing with an unwarranted reservation.

The latter often occurs when the interviewer has made an assumption, often because he's not asked the right question to uncover your experience in a specific area.

Although it's your job to control the interview, there's still a chance that something can get missed, and this is your last opportunity to deal with it.

Be careful, though, not to force-feed information – instead, volunteer to share.

'Thank you for your feedback. You mentioned you have a concern over my international experience. I do have extensive experience working overseas, which we didn't cover in our conversation today, but I would be very happy to share that with you now.'

Ask for a business card, and always follow up

Success at interview is not only about demonstrating your experience; it's also about building a relationship.

Keeping this relationship alive and building on it after the interview is one of the most powerful ways you can stand out from your competition.

Asking for a business card is not only a professional thing to do; it also gives you direct contact details for the interviewer. On receipt, there is implicit permission granted for you to get in touch.

Sending a quick note via e-mail thanking the interviewer for his time and saying how much you enjoyed the interview is a good idea – it goes that extra mile to show you're serious about the position and very keen to work for the organisation.

If you can include something that builds on your conversation that the interviewer may find interesting, then include it. This could be an attached article or a website link to something industry specific that was touched on at the interview. It shows you are thinking and goes that extra step in making you stand out from your competition.

If the interviewer is on LinkedIn, you can send a LinkedIn connection request and a personal message. This approach encourages the interviewer to view your experience once again, so make sure your profile is as good as it can be.

The different interview stages

You now have the opportunity to control the interview at any stage of the process, whether it's your first, second or even third interview.

Your power and ability to do this grows throughout the recruitment process as you learn more about the organisation and the individual or individuals making the decisions.

It all starts with thorough research of the organisation, the interviewer and you, followed by strategic application of this knowledge on the day of the interview.

The way most hiring decisions are made

We've already discussed confidence and preparation as key ingredients for interview success. There is also a third ingredient, which is extremely important at the senior executive level. This is gut feel – more specifically, the gut feel of the person interviewing you.

Countless times, sitting between employer and executive jobseeker while running my own recruitment company, the final decision to take one candidate over another boiled down to gut feel. It was a feeling my client had about a particular candidate, which she found hard to quantify or explain. Call it intuition, a feeling or whatever – time and time again, it's the backbone of the final hiring decision.

There are three ingredients you can use as an executive jobseeker in addition to the techniques already discussed to control an employer's gut feel about you.

Controlling the interview is the primary tool to influence gut feel, but the 'Triple A' – Authority, Amiability and Attention combine to form the icing on the cake. Let's look at each in detail.

Authority – You have to demonstrate the authority of the person you will become in your next position and not the person you are now.

The president of an organisation should carry herself and behave differently to the vice president. In a crowded room the president should be able to convey her seniority in two ways:

1. The investment she makes in her clothes and personal grooming. Little things count and communicate seniority level through attention to detail.

I used to recruit for a very senior individual who was CFO of a large international IT business. Despite his level and experience, what was immediately noticeable was the quality of his clothes. Despite having huge responsibility, he lost power through the way he dressed – he became known as the 'man in the cheap suit'.

2. How she speaks, specifically her tone and speed. Important people tend to speak more slowly; they pause and have the listener hanging on their every word.

To improve this, think about taking a course in presentation skills or join a local public speaking group – remember, conscious practice forms a new empowered habit.

Amiability – Authority needs careful dilution through amiability. This starts with a smile, a shared joke and a genuine interest in the person you are talking to.

People want to work with people they find friendly and pleasant – if you can be respected and liked, then so much the better.

Be yourself and never be afraid to let your personality shine through – this makes you stand out!

Attention – This boils down to listening skills and eye contact. Intuitively we all know when someone is not in the moment with us. We might not consciously tune into this, but our subconscious will tell us in our gut.

In the psychology chapter I advised to practice detachment – to detach from the past and also the future. This enables you to capitalise on the opportunity right in front of you!

I find nothing more off-putting than being in the company of someone who is preoccupied with someone or something else. Even if I respect and like them, if they don't give me the attention we all deserve, my gut feel about them will not be good.

The above form a three-legged stool – take one away, and the thing falls down.

Each must exist in its own right but also in balance and harmony with the other two.

Gut feel is hugely important. It has nothing to do with your skills and experience and very little to do with what you say or don't say.

It's instead about how great and comfortable someone feels in your presence.

While it might be something you've not considered important before, with a little practice, you have the power to influence it.

Interview FAQs

I've heard about these things called competency-based interviews – what are they, and should I be worried?

Competency-based interviews are nothing to be feared – they're just a style of interviewing that has become popular in recent years.

Each question is designed to explore and gain evidence of particular skills and experience.

They are sometimes very open-ended questions, which can lead unwary candidates to waffle and miss the point.

We looked earlier at how to tell great stories with achievements in written form.

It's the same advice in person when communicating verbally – you need a *start, middle* and impactful *end*.

Start – Set the scene of the situation you faced.

Middle – Explain what you did individually or as part of a team to address this situation.

End – Quantify the outcome and value added, using numbers to support where possible.

As in the written form (achievements on your CV), if communicated well, you need one sentence for each – any more than that and you run the risk of waffling.

Interviewers often use a competency-based style of questioning to explore achievements on your CV. It's therefore really important to pick the best achievements and the ones you are comfortable talking about when putting together this document.

What about group interviews or assessment centres – how should I tackle these?

The only difference between a one-on-one interview and a group interview or assessment centre is that you're not alone.

There are usually multiple assessors who observe you, and the group completes an exercise or task to see how you interact and work as a team.

Group interviews or assessment centres usually occur for two reasons:

1. The business hasn't the time to interview all applicants individually, so the assessment centre is a first filter.

2. There is a specific need to see how you interact with others, which could be a specific requirement of the position.

It's usual for the assessment centre to culminate with a shortlist of candidates being taken forward to the one-on-one interview stage.

They're absolutely nothing to fear, and everything we've covered still applies in a group environment.

STEP FIVE:

THE ONLINE EXECUTIVE

You now understand employers' three conversations when hiring and the existence of the hidden market. The Internet has completely changed the executive job market environment for everyone. It's given executive jobseekers even more power to shape their fortune and professional recruiters and employers more tools and opportunities to find the talent they're looking for.

As I said in my first book, *Super Secrets of the Successful Jobseeker*: 'If you don't exist in cyberspace, you don't exist at all.'

In this section, we'll look at the power of your online presence. Starting with an explanation of some of the major platforms, I'll outline key principles to enable you to develop your own social media strategy as part of your personal executive jobseeker plan.

Social media platforms

There are now a multitude of platforms that exist to enable you, the executive jobseeker, to communicate with anyone and everyone at any time you choose.

It's impossible to create and effectively manage a presence on every single social media channel.

What's more important is to pick a few you feel comfortable with and then work them effectively and consistently to your advantage as part of your daily action plan.

Some of the popular platforms, and the ones I tend to favour, include the following:

LinkedIn – linkedin.com

Twitter – twitter.com

Google+ – plus.google.com

Facebook – facebook.com

Pinterest – pinterest.com

Let's look at each of these in greater detail:

LinkedIn

When people talk about social media and the business of finding an executive position online, LinkedIn is often the first platform that springs to mind.

Launched in 2003 as a professional networking platform, it has since been adopted by employers and professional recruiters alike as a primary and cost-effective tool to research, identify and source individuals with the right skills and experience for their business or their clients' businesses.

Twitter

Launched in 2006, Twitter is an online social networking and microblogging service that enables users to send and read short, 140-character messages.

It plays an important part in any executive jobseeker's arsenal but tends to be less understood.

Given its 140-character restriction, Twitter is in my opinion, less versatile than LinkedIn.

Google+

Launched in 2011, Google+ is regarded by some as Google's response to Facebook.

In my own experience, it's far more complicated and less

readily understood than other social media platforms.

However, as Google runs the Internet, there is some validity to the argument that to be found easily online, you should have a Google+ account as part of your social media strategy.

Facebook

In the world of social media, it's hard to escape Facebook. Founded in 2004, it's an online social networking service and provides a forum to share personal information, photographs and videos with friends worldwide.

It's less important than other social media platforms to an executive jobseeker for the purposes of finding a position (to some extent, LinkedIn is regarded as the professional version of Facebook), but it can't be ignored.

Often employers and recruiters cross-reference an executive jobseeker's application to his or her Facebook account because it can provide hints as to what a person is really like away from the work environment.

In addition, just as an employer requests references from previous employers (usually at offer stage), Facebook provides an insightful, cost-effective and extremely useful referencing tool.

Although you may not use Facebook as a proactive executive job search tool, remember that it's online, and what it portrays about you can affect your success in the executive job market.

Pinterest

Pinterest is an online scrapbook that enables users to categorise and organise interesting articles and content found online.

For you as an executive jobseeker, this can be a very useful tool to collate information on a particular company or industry sector as part of your research to access the hidden market.

If you're in a creative industry, it's also a great place to display a portfolio of your work.

A number of key principles are common to the use of all social media platforms. These principles are extremely important and form the foundations of using social media effectively. Let's look at each in turn.

You're being watched

In the past, as an executive jobseeker, you could choose whether to apply for a position you'd seen advertised and whether to register with a particular recruitment business – it was one-way traffic.

Having an online presence changes this, giving organisations an opportunity to contact you directly, whether you have knowledge of or previous experience with them or not.

If you have an online presence, you're being watched whether you like it or not!

Employers are extremely cost conscious in their decision to hire. Appointing a recruitment company or placing an advert on an executive job board involves paying a fee.

Now, through social media, employers of any shape and size have at their fingertips the opportunity to source candidates directly who may be right for their organisations.

Employers now have an alternative outside of their peer group and associate network to find the talent they're looking for. This can be a low-cost option and still comes with an implicit recommendation through mutual connections or actual recommendations online.

The hidden market not only exists but has grown and continues to grow, making it even more important that you as an executive jobseeker learn how to proactively access it.

Many large organisations now have dedicated resourcing teams whose sole job is to proactively scour the Internet for talent.

Similarly, professional recruiters who previously relied on reactive strategies, including candidates responding to advertisements or walking through their door, now have an opportunity to proactively target and engage with anyone they choose.

Everything's faster and nobody's passive

Social media is fast and enables instantaneous communication between two parties regardless of where they're based.

In the past, executive recruiters and employers would place adverts and wait for the response. This could take time – and what if the best candidate in the market didn't see the advert and therefore didn't respond?

Through social media, both parties have the opportunity to contact not only active candidates but also passive executive jobseekers with the right skills and experience for their organisation. What's more, they have the opportunity to do this instantaneously in real time.

Whether you're active in the executive job market or not, if you exist on social media channels, you're highly likely to be approached at some point about executive job opportunities.

Two-way conversation

Social media is all about two-way conversation. Whereas traditional advertising is one-way traffic, social media is about dialogue and actively encourages communication between individuals with similar interests and outlooks.

Embracing social media is therefore not just about being online for the sake of it. It's about having a presence to facilitate communication through asking questions, making comments and giving feedback.

More than just a shop window

Many executive jobseekers look at me blankly when I first ask them in what ways they are proactively using social media to uncover career opportunities and to gain an advantage over their competition.

Most of them know that having a LinkedIn profile is something they need as part of their overall executive job search strategy. Following what others are doing, they create a profile but then do nothing with it.

What they don't appreciate is that to be really successful in uncovering opportunities in the executive job market, they have to actively work their social media profiles on a daily basis.

A social media profile can and should be much more than a shop window to your skills and experience. Just as creating a CV but doing nothing with it is no route to success, creating an online profile but not working that profile proactively is a wasted opportunity.

Route to a face-to-face meeting

The purpose of your CV is to get you an interview. Likewise, the purpose of engaging in social media is not to stay on social media forever but rather to get you a face-to-face meeting with a prospective employer.

In the modern world, it can be tempting to stay behind your computer screen – it feels safe and secure. However, standing out from other executive jobseekers requires some initial discomfort – something that soon disappears and inevitably leads to better results.

Recruitment will always be about people and personalities. To secure the executive position you deserve, you need to get face to face with a prospective employer, and social media is an important tool to help you get there.

Keywords are crucial

Professional recruiters and organisations looking for particular skills and experience have the ability to search online. Social media platforms sit on the Internet, and as such they are searchable, too.

Knowing what someone is likely to type into a Google search or an Advanced People Search on LinkedIn (see later) puts you, the executive jobseeker, at a distinct advantage.

Displaying highly searched keywords on your social media profiles gives you a much higher probability of being found.

Although you may have an idea of what these keywords could be, taking the time to do the following to confirm your thoughts or to identify hidden opportunities is best practice:

Ask – Talk to a professional recruiter who specialises in placing candidates in your sector and at your level. Ask him what he would search online to find someone with your skills and experience.

Job specifications and executive job board adverts – Viewing a number of these in your industry sector and at your level, compiled by both executive recruiters and employers, may yield additional clues as to what's important to them – and therefore important for you to know.

Content is king

Although cramming your profile full of keywords may sound like a good idea, it can have a detrimental impact on your executive job search.

Your social media profiles must be inviting and easy to read.

A number of carefully selected keywords interwoven into an individual profile is your aim, as opposed to a keyword-rich profile that is very difficult to read.

Useful and enticing content that sets you apart from other executive jobseekers draws interest and engagement. For example, LinkedIn published posts give you an opportunity to create useful and engaging content and have an opinion on things happening in your industry sector.

The top priority of Internet search engines is to serve up relevant content. Their success hinges on their ability to provide what content users are searching for and want. Remember this as you complete your profiles, and be sure that you are providing relevant information online to entice executive recruiters and employers to stop and take notice.

A word of warning – before we delve any further into the world of social media, be careful.

Whatever you put on the Internet – on whatever platform and no matter how protected you think it might be – can often be found!

While your LinkedIn profile may convey the image of an intelligent, professional and trustworthy senior executive, having your Facebook profile say something different about you could have a negative impact on an employer's desire to meet with you.

Employers and recruiters use social media not only as a means to find suitable candidates but also to perform due diligence.

This is one of the reasons that, to find success with social media, less is often more.

While it's tempting to have profiles on multiple platforms to cast a wider net, it becomes increasingly difficult to manage their quantity and quality as well as the relevance of content to your target audience.

Furthermore, content on these platforms is not always narrative you have created yourself. Your friends and contacts have an opportunity (depending on your privacy settings) to comment and add media such as photos and videos that, unless you constantly monitor it, you might never know was there.

As part of your personal executive jobseeker plan, having fewer but consistently monitored profiles yields better results than having multiple platforms over which you have little or no control.

The big two

In my opinion, for the purposes of finding an executive position, LinkedIn and Twitter are the big two.

Better to master these two alone than to embrace all social media platforms with minimal effect.

We'll now take a closer look at the big two and how to use them effectively as part of your executive job search strategy.

Everything changes

I regularly log into LinkedIn to find something's changed. Things are in a slightly different place, a new feature has been added or something has been removed.

The world of social media is a competitive environment, and the platforms are constantly developing and evolving to meet the needs of their customers.

Printed text providing detailed guidance on the specifics of each platform can quickly become outdated.

LinkedIn and Twitter have really useful help centres that teach you everything you need to know about how to set up your profile.

What these help centres don't do, though, is show you how to maximise your LinkedIn and Twitter profiles for the executive job market.

For this reason, rather than include step-by-step instructions, which run the risk of becoming obsolete, I'll highlight the key things to create a fantastic LinkedIn and Twitter profile and then, more importantly, show you how to use these profiles to gain an advantage in your executive job search.

We'll look at two aspects of both platforms:

1. Shop Window (SW) – a primarily *reactive* approach.

2. Proactive Engagement Tool (PET) – a primarily *proactive* approach.

But first a bit of background on marketing. In modern marketing, the distinction between SW and PET has become slightly blurred.

Traditionally, marketing's role through advertising, press and media was to engage new customers and persuade them to purchase the products or services that the company was offering.

This worked for a time, but as more and more companies spent time and money on marketing, success meant having the biggest pockets and, subsequently, the loudest voice.

Today as consumers – and for our own self-protection – we've learnt to ignore much of this marketing information and place little reliance on its ability to educate and inform.

Modern marketing understands that through the Internet, buyers are now able to do their own research ahead of any purchase and are much better informed.

Therefore, marketing professionals are placing increasing emphasis on the creation of informative and helpful online content to help potential buyers make their purchasing decisions.

It's a similar story for the modern executive jobseeker. To use social media effectively means creating informative and interesting content for the potential purchasers of your skills and experience.

Success comes from positioning yourself as both knowledgeable and interested in your chosen profession.

Therefore, by definition, SW is about creating your online profile in its static form to attract professional recruiters and employers – *it's predominantly* **reactive** *to what comes your way.* (To draw a parallel with your CV, it's about writing the best CV you possibly can to highlight your skills and experience.)

PET is about supercharging your SW with new and interesting content and making connections with potential employers through common interest – *it's predominantly* **proactive** *in engaging your target audience.*

(To draw a parallel with your CV, it's about taking your CV to where employers and executive recruiters are searching for you online.)

This distinction, while subtle, is extremely important!

LinkedIn

Shop Window (SW)

Photo: Unlike your CV, your LinkedIn profile must have a professional headshot photo. First impressions count – how you look, what you're wearing and the expression on your face all send subliminal messages to the person viewing your profile.

It's not a photo of you on holiday, with the family or on a night out – it's a professional photo in business attire with your hair combed and a smile on your face.

Professional headline: This is a summary of all you are and all you have to offer. Just as a news headline summarises what a particular news story is about, your headline is a snapshot introduction to what follows.

Think keywords here – namely, what professional recruiters and employers will be searching on to find you.

Contact information: Hidden behind a tab is a place to highlight your contact details, which include e-mail address, phone number, location, Twitter accounts and relevant websites. The latter could be the website of the company you currently work for or – better still – your own personal blog.

Public profile: This is your own personal URL, the link to your

LinkedIn profile page that you can share with others. LinkedIn gives you a default URL when you create your profile, but you have the opportunity to change it and make it specific to you.

Mine is https://www.linkedin.com/in/simongrayaca

Because my name is in the URL, chances are high that if someone searches for me on Google, I will be at the top of the search results.

You can change this through Privacy and Settings, where it's also important to make your public profile visible to everyone – it's no good having a fantastic profile if you're invisible to the outside world.

Summary and experience: This is where you document the companies you've worked for and the positions you've held within these organisations. This is effectively an online version of your CV. The same rules that apply in creating a fantastic CV also apply here.

The slight difference here is that you must always be thinking about the words and phrases somebody searching for your skills and experience would be using.

As with a Google search, having the right keywords (the words and phrases you want to be associated with) is essential to ensuring you are approached ahead of your competition.

Skills: You have the option to select up to 50 skills relevant to your experience and expertise.

As with keywords, these are the things you want to be identified with and that viewers of your profile can endorse you for, adding third-party verification that you actually possess these skills.

Interests: As with a CV, including hobbies and interests is very important on your LinkedIn profile. It gives you an opportunity to publish your interests, which can be a useful talking point as part of an initial engagement with a new connection.

Advice for contacting: Under additional information at the bottom of your profile, there is space to provide a message to people who may wish to contact you.

It's important here to explain the things you wish to be contacted for and to once again include your contact details.

Proactive Engagement Tool (PET)

Make connections: Making connections is the key to success on LinkedIn. The more connections you have, the more people you can see and the more people can see you.

Not only the number of connections but also the quality of those connections is important.

On LinkedIn, there are three types of connections:

1. First-degree – people connected to you directly.

2. Second-degree – people your first-degree connections are connected to.

3. Third-degree – people your second-degree connections are connected to.

The wider your connectivity, the greater the number of people you can see and be seen by through the platform.

However, having purely random connections is not as effective as having connections in the industry or sector where you are looking to find your next executive position.

If you are looking for a job in data analytics, 100 connections with senior people in the data analytics industry are far more useful and powerful than 1,000 random connections.

There is much debate about whether you should connect to people you don't know. Much depends on what you're using LinkedIn for, but if your intention is to be found by people who are interested in your skills and experience and in potentially hiring you, such people may well be individuals you don't currently know.

I personally accept LinkedIn connection requests from people I don't know. This is part of my strategy to build a wider reach and level of influence online. On occasion a new connection has sent me unsolicited mail through the platform – when this happens, I simply block that user.

The power of groups: Groups are the most powerful vehicle on LinkedIn for building like-minded connections and finding executive career opportunities. They consist of a collection of individuals on LinkedIn with a common interest, skill or purpose.

Groups are like ponds where employers and recruiters regularly cast their lines in search of a particular type of fish.

You need to make sure you're swimming in the right pond to get caught by the right fisherman!

To give a real-life example; I was once asked to recruit a senior IT auditor for a large international manufacturing organisation.

I posted this opportunity in a group on LinkedIn for IT Audit and was contacted by four relevant candidates. Neil was one of the four. He was ultimately offered and he accepted the position.

If he hadn't been a member of this group, it's unlikely I'd have found him, and he wouldn't be where he is today!

There's another benefit to joining groups. By default, joining a group gives you a group connection to everyone else in that group. It increases your visibility on the platform and gives you the opportunity to message other group members.

Recommendations: LinkedIn gives you something extremely powerful – recommendations – that a CV generally doesn't. Recommendations are an important third-party verification of all you claim on your LinkedIn profile.

They are attached to specific companies and add validity to your skills and experience because you don't write them.

For you to say how great you are is one thing, but for somebody else to endorse what you claim has far greater impact and is something both employers and professional recruiters actively look for.

On LinkedIn, the more quality recommendations you have, the more assurance you give a potential employer over the decision to approach you and potentially hire you. This carries even more weight if the person who recommended you is someone he or she actually knows and trusts.

Advanced People Search: This is LinkedIn's search tool and is very useful for helping you to identify and get in front of the decision maker in addition to preparing for interview.

As part of your targeted approach to the hidden market, you can identify individuals by keywords, job title, company and geographical area.

For example, searching for *retail* within a 15-mile radius of your postcode gives you search results for anyone with a connection to the retail sector in your locality.

This tool is hugely powerful for finding organisations and contacts within these organisations as part of your plan to attack the hidden market.

This is where the power of groups comes fully into play. For example, through my Advanced People Search, I find Jenny, the director of a retail business I'm keen to approach. I'm not connected to Jenny, we've never done business together, and we're not friends. I also don't know her e-mail address.

Without using InMail (a paid service on the platform), LinkedIn makes it difficult for me to connect.

However, scrolling down Jenny's profile, I notice that she is a member of an open group called The Retail Network.

If I now request to join this group and am accepted, from LinkedIn's perspective I now have something in common with Jenny. I now have the option to message her directly through the group.

Sharing updates: LinkedIn gives you the opportunity to share updates with your connections or the public at large. It gives you a voice on the platform to talk about things you have an opinion on and to share useful and interesting content that you or others have created. For an executive jobseeker, this is a powerful tool.

Peter is looking for an opportunity in the aerospace industry and has built a reputation on LinkedIn for sharing useful content on everything aerospace.

Through regular updates, he has become a focal point for knowledge on the aerospace industry and as such is more likely to be found by those looking to hire into this sector.

Demonstrating your work: Sometimes demonstrating what

you've done is far easier than explaining it. This is particularly true in the creative industries. For example, if you're an artist, it's far easier to display your pictures than to try to explain them through words.

LinkedIn enables you to add a video, image or document (hosted by one of their supported providers) to your profile summary or to any of your individual roles.

SlideShare (slideshare.net) is one such supported provider and allows you to update files in a variety of formats, pulling these through to your LinkedIn profile.

In addition to displaying your work, it also breaks up the text with interesting and engaging visual content.

This gives your profile stickiness. People are more likely to stop, take notice and have a good look around.

Published posts: LinkedIn also gives you an opportunity to create and publish posts. This is essentially blogging, which is one of the most powerful tools in driving traffic to websites and to your LinkedIn profile.

Your published posts sit in a prominent position at the top of your profile just below your contact information.

For example, looking for an opportunity in the aerospace industry, Peter discusses issues relevant to this sector in his published posts, which are interesting and informative.

Peter has created a name for himself as someone not only interested in aerospace but also very knowledgeable about current issues.

Pulse: LinkedIn Pulse is an application that enables you to follow specific topics that you're interested in.

If you're interested in technology, you can follow the technology channel, or if you're interested in business, you can follow the business channel.

Similarly, you can follow influencers, who are essentially high-level marketmakers – well-connected individuals in a particular subject area or industry space.

Influencers, if approached in the right way (in line with the executive jobseeker dichotomy), could be extremely powerful in helping you find the executive position you deserve.

LinkedIn Pulse collates information about what and whom you are interested in under Your News. It's a great source of content to share through your status updates or to comment on in your published posts.

Twitter

Shop Window (SW)

Compared to LinkedIn, creating a Twitter profile is much easier with fewer fields to complete.

You'll need a photo and a brief biography, but that's about it.

Twitter is primarily used as a PET through regular interaction and engagement.

Proactive Engagement Tool (PET)

Tweets: Twitter is all about tweets. It's about creating or identifying interesting content and sharing this across the platform.

Following: By following key influencers or companies (denoted by the @ symbol) in your sector, you can obtain valuable and up-to-date information on what's happening, what's important and things you should know.

Followers: By composing regular tweets on topics relating to your industry sector, you encourage people to follow you. The more followers, the more reach you have, in a similar vein to LinkedIn connections.

Hashtags (#): By searching on tagged topics (e.g. #aerospace), you uncover recent posts in which users have tagged their tweets as being important or relevant to the aerospace sector. This is useful for uncovering hot topics and identifying businesses or individuals worth approaching.

Retweets (RT): You don't need to be the original creator of all content you share on Twitter. When you RT someone else's post, it appears in your feed and is visible to all of your followers (very similar to LinkedIn's Share feature). It tells the content creator that you like what she's said and can be a starting point for further more meaningful communication.

A word of warning – be careful what you RT because your followers will rarely make the distinction between your original content and what you've shared. To them, it's all your opinion, so be careful what you put your name to.

Favourite: If you favourite a post (very similar to LinkedIn's Like feature), you're giving a thumbs-up.

Not quite as strong as a RT, it still has power and sends a positive message to the content creator.

Lists: This feature enables you to create lists on any topic you choose. For example, if you have identified 20 businesses in the retail sector that you want to keep a close eye on, you can create a specific list for them.

You can do the same for key marketmakers or industry associations.

Lists keep things organised and are a way to keep watch without openly following an individual or organisation.

Direct messages (DM): If you follow someone who follows you, Twitter allows you to send the individual a DM. Having built engagement and trust through a series of communications, you can request further communication offline by exchanging contact details privately.

At some point, taking things offline is a good idea due to Twitter's 140-character restriction, which will take any conversation only so far!

STEP SIX:

EFFECTIVE EXECUTIVE NETWORKING

Networking is the thing that executive jobseekers often fear the most. It can bring to mind a roomful of strangers handing out business cards and making small talk.

It's true that many networking events are run this way. People just turn up and engage in trivial conversation without any real strategy or direction as to what they're looking to achieve.

While this type of activity is labelled networking by many, effective executive networking is something completely different and is a powerful tool to stand out from the competition and to uncover executive opportunities that exist only in the hidden market.

Principles

Before we get into the details, it's important to highlight some key principles of effective executive networking.

It's where high-probability executive job opportunities exist

You now understand the three conversations that someone looking to hire has with his or her peer group, extended network and ultimately executive job boards or professional recruiters.

The preference is often to hire through the peer group or extended network for two reasons:

1. There is no financial outlay because there isn't an executive job board or professional recruiter to pay.

2. Any introduction comes with an implicit recommendation. People usually only recommend someone they know, trust, or at least have heard good things about – anything less than this may end up reflecting very badly on them at some point.

The conversations that happen within peer groups and extended networks reveal the hidden market. This is where a high number of executive job opportunities exist and are ultimately filled – but most executive jobseekers never ever see.

Networking gives you, the executive jobseeker, the opportunity to access the hidden market and to uncover high-probability career opportunities before they are ever advertised to the masses. It's your opportunity to get ahead of the game.

As you discovered earlier, accessing the hidden market requires more effort and time investment than applying to an executive job advert online or registering with a recruitment company, but it's worth it!

It's uncomfortable for a reason

The fact that most executive jobseekers find networking uncomfortable is great news.

If something is uncomfortable, it means it's less likely to be done; thus, your competition is less likely to be doing one of the most important things for finding success in today's competitive executive job market.

Adrian, a good friend of mine, has a saying that the universe has a habit of showing up with something uncomfortable when you're ready to move to the next stage of your journey in life. This 'something uncomfortable' is absolutely the thing you should be doing. If we as human beings all stayed within our comfort zones, there would be no advancement and no personal development. Many of the things we have come to rely on as part of our everyday lives would never have been invented.

Success in all walks of life comes down to your belief systems. If you believe that networking is difficult, you'll be less likely to take action.

On the other hand, if through your understanding of the executive job market environment you believe that networking is a direct route to access the hidden market (which it absolutely is), then despite the initial discomfort, you will take positive and proactive action to do it.

However, even with empowered belief systems, executive jobseekers can still find networking a challenge for two reasons:

1. *They have no strategy*: You need a plan of attack to be successful at networking. Knowing what your goal is for any individual networking event enables you to put a strategy and clearly defined actions in place to deliver that goal.

2. *They don't do it often enough*: When you first go to the gym after a long break, you're likely to ache for a few days afterwards. The more regularly you go, the more you get used to it and the stronger and fitter you become. Getting better at networking is like exercising a muscle; you need to do it consistently and regularly.

It's the culmination of all you've learnt thus far

Effective executive networking combines much of what we've discussed in this book so far and is one of the most effective ways to access the hidden market, where a high proportion of high-probability executive opportunities always exist.

The starting point for most executive jobseekers is executive job boards and professional recruiters – they never uncover the hidden market.

Through a lack of knowledge, education and effort, they decide to take their chances with everyone else and then wonder why finding the executive position of their dreams takes so long, if it ever happens at all.

You're now aware of the existence of marketmakers, who are the fifth participant and a significant player in the executive job market.

The successful executive jobseeker puts considerable effort into going directly to the employer and leveraging the power of marketmakers – doing what the masses aren't doing and, as a minority, securing the lion's share of success.

Marketmakers are influential figures within an industry sector who are well known, are well respected and possess an enviable contact book. They are extremely comfortable in social environments and, by the very nature of who they are, what they do and what they enjoy, can often be found at networking events.

If you don't go to networking events, you're unlikely to meet them and therefore will miss out on a key route to find the executive position you're looking for.

Effective executive networking is all about marketmakers, who – given the right circumstances – will introduce you to people who can offer you an executive position in the hidden market…but they won't do this right away.

Because marketmakers participate in conversations with trusted peers and business associates, they don't give recommendations lightly.

As an executive jobseeker, it's important to build relationships with them over a period of time. Investing this time with a well-connected marketmaker can lead to significant payoffs – maybe not today, but very likely at some point in the not-too-distant future.

The next time someone approaches a marketmaker and asks him whom he knows or can recommend, there's a high probability of him thinking of you first!

It's not about meeting someone looking to hire

It is highly unlikely that you will bump into someone at a networking event who is looking to hire someone with your skills and experience at that precise moment in time.

Unfortunately, many executive jobseekers believe this is the case, and when they don't happen upon someone who is ready to hire them on the spot, they lose interest in that particular conversation, also losing the desire to attend future networking events.

You can see in their eyes and in their body language that they've concluded the person they're talking to doesn't currently have a vacant position at their level. So they turn away and make an excuse, and it's off to the next disempowered conversation.

Little do they know that they've left someone extremely well connected in their industry space that on a regular basis meets individuals and organisations that may have a need and desire for their skills.

If only they'd stayed a little longer and had a more empowered and mutually beneficial conversation, this marketmaker might just have recommended them the next time he was asked whom he could recommend.

It's not about selling

Remember the executive jobseeker dichotomy, one of the most important principles in the Career Codex methodology and a framework for all communication and engagement with yourself and the outside world?

As a quick reminder:

Your success in the executive job market has nothing to do with the executive job market itself; it has everything to do with you.

In all communication with professional recruiters, employers, and marketmakers, it's never about you; it's always about them.

At networking events, the same holds true – it's never about selling. The sad irony, however, is that because many executive jobseekers believe it is about selling (something they're uncomfortable doing), networking is perceived as difficult and often avoided.

In *Super Secrets of the Successful Jobseeker*, I introduced two couples – Mr and Mrs HAMBUC and Mr and Mrs ALSIC.

Both couples are uncomfortable going to networking events alone, so they travel in pairs. This means that at least they have the option of just talking to one another – and because this is the easier option, they often do!

The HAMBUCs (**H**and out **A**ll **M**y **BU**siness **C**ards) hand out business cards and collect business cards from everyone they meet. The more cards they obtain, the more successful they deem the networking event to have been. Unfortunately, exchanging business cards does not mean they've built a meaningful relationship with someone who could recommend them; it simply means they've exchanged business cards!

The ALSICs (**A**rrive **L**ate and **S**tand **I**n the **C**orner) arriving late and standing in the corner TOGETHER, miss the whole point of networking – talking to people they don't yet know!

Don't be a HAMBUC or an ALSIC, but have fun watching them work at the next networking event you attend.

As I often say, observing the actions of others is sometimes the most powerful but most underutilised source of education for our own personal development.

Everyone is in the same boat

As human beings, we have a habit of convincing ourselves that we're the only one. We're the only one having a bad day, we're the only one stuck in traffic or we're the only one who feels uncomfortable or out of place at a networking event. This is simply not the case.

Everyone is in the same boat and worries beforehand whether he or she will find someone to talk to and what the event will be like.

Understanding this should reassure you that making the first move to engage a stranger in conversation is likely to receive a welcoming response.

What is effective executive networking?

Effective executive networking is about mutually beneficial conversations. It's about listening and not talking at people, and it's about taking an interest in others and what they do.

It's a prelude to building meaningful relationships over time, which requires subsequent and reasonably regular meetings. If you want someone to remember you and recommend you, you have to put in the time and effort.

When I ran my recruitment company, I would attend regular networking events.

One particular event that springs to mind is a breakfast seminar I attended run by the IoD (Institute of Directors), where I bumped into a lawyer named Simon.

I asked Simon open questions about his organisation, what he did and what mattered to him. I asked him what an ideal client looked like to him and what projects he was currently working on.

Using the principles of the executive jobseeker dichotomy, it was all about him. I gave him a forum to talk about himself without even initially mentioning who I was and what I did – this was key to building rapport with Simon.

The best conversations are always two-way interactions, and as our conversation naturally progressed, Simon asked me what I did.

This was my opportunity to tell him a bit more about me and my business.

Rather than telling him I was a recruitment consultant (a surefire way to end the conversation), I told him the story of a recent recruitment assignment I'd worked on for a service sector client.

As with powerful achievements on a super executive CV, this story had a start, middle and end. In telling this story, I demonstrated to Simon how I worked and how I'd added value to a client.

Through the context of my story, I helped him to remember what I did and gave him a vehicle to communicate it to others – storytelling really is that powerful!

At the end of the event, I went up to Simon to say goodbye and only then exchanged business cards. Back at my office, I dropped him a line via e-mail to say how much I'd enjoyed our conversation, and I suggested that we get together for a coffee.

We did just that and started a business relationship that resulted in Simon introducing me to other senior figures in his law firm and directly referring business to me.

Planning for success

There are a few things to consider before attending any networking event:

- *Who?*
- *Where?*
- *How?*
- *How often?*

Let's explore the significance of each in greater detail:

Who?

We've covered this already – the 'who' is marketmakers who have the power to introduce and recommend. The more specific the networking event is to your industry sector, the more likely it is that the people you meet will have extensive contacts in your sector of choice.

For example, if I attend a networking event run by ICAEW (Institute of Chartered Accountants in England and Wales), I have a good chance of bumping into marketmakers who have a particular interest and contact base in the accountancy world. If I'm looking for a senior position in finance, this is the type of focused networking event I should definitely attend.

Remember, you're not there to meet someone who will offer you an executive position right now – you're there to build effective relationships.

Where?

There are so many networking events these days, but it's hard to know which to attend. Indeed, networking events have become a big business, with individuals making a living from organising them.

If you wanted to, you could probably network morning, noon and night, but you'd do little else besides!

Networking requires energy, and as human beings, we all have a limited amount of energy we can put to good use on any particular day.

I like to draw a comparison with the fuel tank in a car. If we have ample fuel, we run well and perform to the best of our ability. However, if we're down to the fumes, then naturally our performance is negatively affected. Despite our best efforts, if we're not at our best, our results will be compromised.

This means you have to be selective in the networking events you attend. Your investment time will determine the number of events you can go to in any one week, but the most important question to ask is how many *relevant* events you can attend while maintaining your *productivity* as part of a balanced portfolio of activity.

To decide whether to attend a particular networking event, ask yourself the following three questions:

1. Where is it located?

If you're looking for an executive position in a particular geographical location, then it's a good idea to focus your networking efforts in that particular region.

If you're looking for a job in Nottingham, although attending a networking event in London might yield some benefits, there are likely to be more Nottingham-based marketmakers at an event located in Nottingham.

The exception to this rule would be a large industry-specific conference that draws delegates from far and wide to a central location. If it's industry specific, it might just be worth that extra bit of effort, wherever it's based.

Even if you're not restricted geographically, it's a good idea to focus on one particular geographical area at a time. If you cast your net too wide, you're likely to catch nothing.

2. Why am I going?

Going to a networking event purely for networking can be a reason in itself, but it helps if there's a bit more.

If the event has an educational element, includes an interesting speaker or covers a topic you're particularly interested in, then whether you meet an influential marketmaker or not, you're likely to derive some benefit.

Also, listening collectively to a speaker can serve as a fantastic icebreaker to get the conversation flowing once formal proceedings are over.

For example:

'I really enjoyed hearing Tom present today. Have you heard him speak before?'

Bingo! You're already engaged in conversation with somebody you don't know without even trying!

3. Have I been before?

Experience is a great teacher. Even if you make a mistake in your decision to attend a networking event, it can be time well spent providing you don't make the same mistake twice.

Seeking direction in industry publications and from people you know and trust can help you save time in finding the best events.

How?

So how do you make the most of any networking event? You're already miles ahead of your competition in understanding how to network effectively, but to help you further, here are a few of my tried and tested techniques for success:

Be yourself. Trying to be something you're not with people you don't know can be a recipe for disaster, because at some point you'll get found out.

While it's tempting to try to fit in, you now know this is exactly what not to do.

As a senior executive, you'll be expected to have an opinion on certain issues, and even if the people you meet disagree with your viewpoint, they'll respect you for having one.

Remember, we can't all get on with everyone, and we naturally gravitate to certain types of people – that's just life.

Get there early: Arriving before everybody else might seem scary, but it actually makes networking much easier. This is your opportunity to speak to and build a relationship with the organiser(s) of the event – because they're organising, they'll be there even earlier than you.

Think about it; the organiser of the networking event is by definition a very powerful marketmaker, likely to know most of the people attending and with the power to make introductions.

As you're there early, you have the opportunity to look at the list of attendees and to plan whom in the room you'd like to meet during the event.

Let the organiser know why you're there, and ask him or her to recommend people you should speak to. Better still, ask for an introduction!

Simply standing next to the organiser as guests arrive gives you perceived power. Attendees will assume you are well connected and are likely to seek you out to engage in conversation as part of their own networking strategy.

Be patient: Networking is not a race; it's about engaging in conversation and building relationships. Take the time to listen to others before discussing your own reasons for being there. This builds rapport and leads to more empowered conversations.

By listening first and talking second, you gain the opportunity to find out about the person you're speaking with. When it's your turn to speak, you are then better able to position the conversation so it's most relevant to the listener.

Never, ever dive in and tell the person you're speaking with that you're looking for a job. Your search for an executive position doesn't define you – your skills, experience and personality do.

When it's your turn to speak, tell the story of a recent achievement or accomplishment and tag onto the end of this that you're currently in the executive job market and considering opportunities. Don't make the fact that you're looking for a position the only thing you have to say.

Follow up: Meeting at a networking event is not the finish but rather the start of a new relationship. You must be prepared to follow up.

Sending an e-mail to someone you met to thank her for her time and to say how much you enjoyed her company is an absolute must. In addition, referencing something she said in discussion shows you were listening and taking an interest.

Just as I did with Simon, having a follow-up meeting over coffee to build on the initial meeting is what takes the relationship to the next level.

How often?

As already mentioned, the number of networking events you decide to attend depends on your investment time and energy levels.

Regular and often, as with all things that involve building new habits, is preferential to short bursts of activity that are rarely repeated.

Effective executive networking is about building new beliefs, new thinking and new skills to open doors you never before knew existed.

You don't even need to attend a networking event to practice networking effectively. Get into the habit of striking up conversations with complete strangers in all walks of life as an everyday activity.

When I buy coffee in the morning or fill up at the petrol station, I practice networking.

By asking questions and passing the time of day, you learn the skills to build communication channels and relationships with anyone and everyone.

It's not about clever questions or fancy statements; it's about taking an interest in another person – who they are, what they do and why it matters to them.

And finally, here is the ultimate 'TEC'hnique for building relationships with people you don't know.

Building the trust and the confidence of new acquaintances is key to their taking the risk of referring or recommending you to anyone in their personal network.

TEC stands for Time, Experience and Confirmation.

Time: Building new relationships takes time, and you must be prepared to invest this time. This is why the HAMBUCs fail so miserably at networking – they expect instantaneous business and referrals without doing any of the hard work.

Experience: Linked closely to time is experience. The more often someone can experience you and what you're all about, the better. In addition, the more someone can experience you at different times and across different media, the faster any initial meeting will turn into a meaningful relationship.

For example, someone who met you at a networking event and then subsequently for coffee has more experience with you than someone you've simply handed your business card to.

Confirmation: This is about whom you know in common. If we've just met but we both know Geoff, then this connection in common not only leads to a likely topic of conversation but also builds trust and understanding between us much faster. A great starting point to establishing potential areas of confirmation is through shared connections on LinkedIn.

STEP SEVEN:

INNOVATE TO STAY AHEAD

Throughout the previous chapters of this book, the Career Codex methodology has unfolded to enable you to think and act differently in the executive job market, giving you new ideas and techniques to implement as part of your personal executive jobseeker plan.

Perhaps without knowing it, if you have followed the principles and advice contained within this book, you are already innovating and are several very big steps ahead of your competition for the executive position you want.

Innovation can best be described as a new idea or method put to effective use. To stay ahead of your competition and to avoid being left on the shelf, you have to do it consistently.

Furthermore, in this section, you'll explore how certainty, probability and context play an important role in the workings of the executive job market.

Staying ahead

Now one of your key strengths in the executive job market is your new way of thinking and your ability to do things differently from your competition.

When entering the executive job market, most executive jobseekers copy what other people are doing as if it were a blueprint for success – as you now know, this isn't standing out from the crowd.

Think about it; if there is a job with 100 applicants, it's not the candidate who blends into the background and plays it safe who is going to get noticed. The executive jobseeker that breaks the blueprint to stand out from the crowd is the one most likely to get hired.

Innovation requires that you stay ahead of your competition and that, through the principles and processes outlined in this book, you do this on a daily basis.

This may seem daunting at first (everything does when it's new to you), but the good news is that you are already reprogrammed to innovate consistently and successfully through the power of observation and feedback.

Observation

Instead of looking at the actions of other people as a template for your own activity in the executive job market, always consider things from a different perspective. Question what you observe, and use the actions of others as a valuable addition to your executive jobseeker education and training. If the majority of jobseekers are investing time in the preparation of a perfect CV, what could you do differently?

You now know that there is no such thing as a perfect CV. How better could you spend your time?

The power of innovation is actually not having the right answers at the outset but rather the ability to ask the right questions!

As an example, in my book *Super Secrets of the Successful Jobseeker*, I talk about a concept called 'Race to Face'. This is a concept I developed by observing other people and understanding their limiting beliefs and the action those beliefs had stopped them from taking.

The answer to the question (and ultimately the Race to Face concept) came from asking the right questions in the first place:

How can a jobseeker shorten the time frame between CV submission and interview?

How can a jobseeker increase the probability of being invited in for an interview?

Through the planning process, putting together your destination statement and identifying a number of organisations you would like to work for, putting on your best business attire, printing off a copy of your CV and turning up at an employer's premises can pay dividends.

Most executive jobseekers won't do this. They think they're pestering the employer, and it sits way outside of their comfort zone.

You now know that employers like to hear from you if you approach them in the right way. It saves them time, energy and money when they need to recruit.

Indeed, they sometimes will create an opportunity right now if an individual with the right skills and experience shows up on their doorstep. It may not be a permanent position at the right salary, but it could be an interesting project that leads to a well-paid permanent position further down the track.

You also know that feeling uncomfortable is simply an opportunity to expand your comfort zone. Stepping confidently into the unknown may seem difficult at first, but it is preferable to hunting in the pack and hoping to be the one who gets noticed.

Let's look at a quick example and introduce AJ. AJ knows he'd like to work for P80 Ltd. He knows this because he's done thorough research on the business and on the skills and experience he could potentially offer the organisation.

Arriving at P80 Ltd's reception, he doesn't care whether the company has a current live executive position or not – he's simply there to put himself on the radar of the business both now and for the future.

AJ knows the managing director's name is Sasha Jones. Politely introducing himself to the receptionist, he asks for a moment of Sasha's time.

He explains that he's done extensive research into P80 Ltd (establishing a higher baseline) and was pleased to read about the company's recent contract win. He goes on to say that he's here to offer his enthusiasm, skills and experience to Sasha whether an opportunity exists now or not, and if she's available, he would welcome the opportunity to hand his CV over in person.

What do you think the receptionist is likely to think? If Sasha comes out to meet AJ, what do you think she is likely to think? If nothing else, AJ will be remembered by the receptionist, by Sasha and by P80 Ltd. If nothing is available now, when an opportunity next turns up at a senior level, whom do you think they're likely to contact first?

On paper, AJ might not have been the strongest candidate with the best skills and experience for P80 Ltd, but it doesn't really matter. Understanding that recruitment decisions are often made on gut feel and by playing the game differently, he's put himself in pole position for opportunities now and in the future with the organisation.

This is Race to Face in action and shows how observation can lead to innovation and different action to take you from CV to interview in one hit.

What are you currently observing in the executive job market in your industry sector that could provide you with an opportunity to stand out and take action that is memorable and different from that of everyone else?

Feedback

Feedback is something few executive jobseekers are prepared to ask for because of the risk of what they might hear.

Even when they are brave enough to ask for it, they often make excuses for what's said because they don't understand the power of self-evaluation for self-improvement.

Feedback takes two forms:

First, it's your own analysis and assessment using your thinking journal of how you're acting – and more importantly, how you're thinking in the executive job market.

Second, it's feedback gained from others. This is never feedback to be argued with or challenged – feedback is simply feedback based on somebody else's perception of you.

Being brave means you're prepared to ask for feedback from

executive recruiters, employers, marketmakers and anyone else you come into contact with who can give you a valuable assessment of you and your positioning in the executive job market.

Exploring certainty, probability and context

As human beings, we like certainty – we like to know that if we do **A**, we'll get **B**, something I call the *certainty link*.

The certainty link often determines our level of effort and, ultimately, our attainment of results.

For example, if you believe there are no opportunities in the executive job market and that, therefore, even if you exert effort and take steps to find a position, there is no guarantee of a result, how much effort are you likely to take?

I'd guess not as much as you would if you could be certain of the end result of securing the executive opportunity you want.

The problem here is that expectations can often be self-fulfilling, and this is where the certainty link can cause executive jobseekers a whole host of problems.

Unless they can see a certain result, they take minimal action and as such get the result they thought they would get anyway – crazy, I know, but true!

As you've learned, many executive jobseekers focus their entire job search success on the structure and content of their CV. They obsess over it and write multiple versions based on the inaccurate assumption that the perfect CV is just around the corner. This is an illusion because, however good their CV is, it will not be viewed as good by every single executive recruiter or employer – there is no certainty.

We humans are largely a product of our past, and our perceptions cause us to see things differently from how the next person does. Even two employers in the same business could read an identical CV in a completely different way, with one deciding to interview and the other throwing the CV away – that's just how things work.

This is where innovation comes in. Now that you know there is no perfect way to approach the executive job market and that doing **A** does not guarantee **B**, you have the freedom to experiment.

Innovative thinking and trying new things is part and parcel of successful executive job search and is something to adopt if you want to stand head and shoulders above your competition.

It's your job as a successful executive jobseeker to understand this, to be brave and to experiment with every aspect of your executive job search, learning from the feedback and results you get along the way.

Through the experience of working on your personal executive jobseeker plan, by keeping diligent records in your thinking journal and through being present in the moment to observe your surroundings, you'll get a feel for what works well for you and what doesn't.

With experience, you'll begin to understand probabilities relevant to you, enabling you to do more of what works and less of what doesn't.

To drive the previous point home, let me expand and elaborate on a real-life example I highlighted earlier.

When I ran my own recruitment business and was in the market for hiring a recruitment consultant, I would often give the prospective candidate a challenge ahead of the second interview stage (this was me innovating in how to make a successful hiring decision).

Matt had already approached me in the right way with a well-worded CV and a phone call to follow up, converting his approach into a face-to-face interview.

As he had performed well at our first meeting, I asked him to prepare a letter to one of our target clients before his second interview. The target client I gave him was Punch Taverns plc (one of the UK's largest leased pub companies).

When Matt presented me with his letter at second interview stage as a 'message in a bottle' (a wine bottle with my company's logo on it, with his letter rolled up inside), I was blown away.

To some extent, what the letter said was irrelevant; the message that he was the candidate for the job and the person I had to hire had already been delivered.

In the context of that day and at that time, Matt's message in a bottle worked as planned, and I hired him on the spot!

On a different day, things might not have worked so well. What if I'd gotten up on the wrong side of the bed that morning? What if one of my fellow interviewers hadn't liked the idea for whatever reason? On another day and at another time, Matt might not have achieved the result he was hoping for.

Context is just an extension of probability, which plays an important role in everything. Just because something works today doesn't mean it will work the exact same way all of the time.

I drive to work at the same time along the same road every day. If I really concentrate and there's limited traffic, I can even do this at the same speed and arrive at about the same time.

But when it snows, the probability of my even getting to work (let alone on time) drops considerably. I have a rear-wheel-drive car with a powerful engine, but in the context of snow, a 4x4 would give me a far better chance of getting to work on time and in one piece!

It's difficult to accurately predict the weather. It's even harder to determine how people will react in certain situations, which is further complicated by the fact that the same person may react in different ways on different days and at different times.

Although we as human beings tend to prefer certainty, to find success in the executive job market, you need to exert effort to embrace probability and to understand that probabilities can change from one day to the next depending on the context.

This is why you have a personal executive jobseeker plan that you stick to no matter what.

Your plan is your focus and is the only constant in an environment of ever-changing variables and associated probabilities.

STEP EIGHT:

HANDLING THE OFFER & NEGOTIATION STAGE

The purpose of everything we've covered thus far has been to get you, the executive jobseeker, to offer stage. The offer stage of any recruitment process is the position where an employer decides you are the person he or she wishes to hire.

The employer puts together an offer letter, which contains salary details, benefits and other terms relating to your employment. This is sent to you, and you are given time to consider and to decide whether this is the position you wish to accept.

The power shift

At the offer stage, a power shift takes place. Throughout the recruitment process and certainly up until now, the employer (in his or her mind, at least) has had the power.

Now things have changed – out of all of the people they've considered and interviewed, they've made the decision to choose you.

This puts them in a position of vulnerability for two reasons:

1. You may reject the offer, and unless there is a backup candidate, they could be back to square one.

2. They are no longer in control – the decision-making power and the amount of time this may take has shifted from them to you.

As an executive jobseeker, this is a good position to be in and is the point where many people might be tempted to give a deep sigh of relief and thank their blessings that they've finally been offered a position.

Whether it's a position they actually want is another matter; the point is that typical executive jobseekers have never been in control throughout the recruitment process. Now, having received an offer, they feel relieved, grateful and possibly tempted to accept without further consideration or thought.

Having almost finished reading this book, you now understand that you have been in control of the recruitment process all along. To receive an offer for your efforts is no surprise, and by maintaining control, the knee-jerk reaction to immediately accept is replaced by a detailed consideration of the offer in question and the possibility of negotiating better terms.

Offers are like buses

Think back to your calendar time – the typical amount of time you would expect it to take you to find an executive position given your industry sector and level of seniority.

Having run an effective recruitment process through your personal executive jobseeker plan, as you reach the end of this time period, it should come as no surprise if a number of offers manifest themselves at the same time.

This often causes executive jobseekers a headache – what to do, how to manage the process and how to keep everybody happy?

It's often tempting to bury your head in the sand and ignore calls from professional recruiters or employers who will be chasing to see if you've made a decision.

However, it's not your responsibility to keep everybody happy; it's your responsibility to make the right decision for you and you alone regarding which is the right position to accept and on what terms.

To do this effectively, you need to keep open lines of communication with the executive recruiter or employer so that they know at all times where you are in your decision-making process.

Nothing sets off alarm bells more than an executive jobseeker that doesn't return calls after an offer has been made.

To understand this stage of the recruitment process a little better, let's take a moment to delve into the mind of the professional recruiter and a typical employer after having made an offer.

What the recruiter thinks: Sitting between the employer and you, their candidate, the executive recruiter will normally receive news of the offer from the employer via e-mail or over the telephone.

In my experience, details at this stage can be quite scant. Salary, car allowance and some of the benefits are usually communicated, but there can be holes in the information received.

It's amazing how many of my past clients have been unsure about various details of the remuneration package yet still expected me to field an incomplete offer to my candidate in the hope that he or she would just accept.

The recruitment process will usually have taken far longer than expected, and often the final part of any offer communication is to find out how quickly the chosen candidate can start!

After what could have been months of hard work, the professional recruiter is looking for one thing and one thing only, and that is to get paid.

This could be the recruitment fee in full or, if a proportion of the fee was given along the way in the form of a retainer, the final element (at the senior executive level, this will still be a sizeable amount of money).

Your decision to accept the position or not determines whether the recruiter gets paid. He or she has a vested interest in getting you across the line as quickly as possible.

Not surprisingly and often without conscious thought, such individuals can often put undue pressure on their candidate to accept quickly. They are desperate to chalk up on the offer board in their office that the position has been accepted and to publicly display the fee they've made.

Recruitment is a competitive environment, and despite the advent of technology, many recruitment businesses still use a whiteboard to record accepted offers – it's the scoreboard visible to everyone for that particular month.

In addition to internal pressure to make the fee, the recruiter also faces considerable pressure from their client.

While employers may take months to make decisions on CVs or whom to see for interviews, once they've made up their mind, they want a decision, and they want it now. It's somewhat ironic that they have taken their time yet expect the chosen candidate to make a decision almost instantaneously.

The executive recruiter is therefore under pressure to get a favourable decision. What's more, he or she is under pressure to make things happen right now!

What the employer thinks: It's a similar situation for an employer who hasn't been using a recruitment business and has instead gone to market directly.

Such employers have invested time, effort and energy in the recruitment process. They now want a return on this investment and again will be looking for you to make a favourable decision as quickly as possible.

Let's now take a closer look at the offer and negotiation stage by breaking it down into its component parts:

- Receiving the offer

- Handling the offer

- Negotiating a better offer

Receiving the offer

The executive recruiter or employer will often phone you to give you the good news that you've been offered the position. He or she will probably do this ahead of producing any paperwork in the form of a formal offer letter for two reasons:

1. *People like to give good news.* In my time in recruitment, one of my favourite things to do was to communicate a verbal offer to one of my candidates. Despite the pressure

of not knowing whether he'd accept or not, the mere action of telling him he'd done well and was the chosen candidate was something I really enjoyed.

2. *The sooner they've told you, the sooner they expect you to make a decision.* Waiting for paperwork before they've sown the seed in your head only delays this process. In their mind, the decision clock starts ticking from the moment they've told you rather than from when the paperwork lands.

Handling the offer

Your responsibility as an executive jobseeker is to stay in control of the recruitment process until you've made your decision of whether or not to accept the position.

There are five things you can do to handle the offer effectively while retaining control and giving yourself adequate time to make the right decision:

1. *Thank them.* Acknowledge receipt of the offer with a big thank you, and let the professional recruiter or employer know you are thrilled to be the one selected.

2. *Request the offer in writing.* This is the best way to put the brakes on, giving you breathing space to make a decision. Requesting the offer in writing takes time – time for the employer to complete the paperwork and then to get it out to you.

Whether a recruiter has been involved in the recruitment process or not, the offer letter will usually come directly from the employer. Sometimes the recruiter is copied on this correspondence, but in my experience this rarely happens. The executive recruiter will be managing both the client, to get the letter out as quickly as possible, and also you, to confirm that you've received it.

3. *Clarify.* Having received the offer letter, clarifying various terms gives you a further opportunity to create additional time to make a decision on the offer. This can be particularly important if

you have a number of offers landing at the same time that you wish to compare and contrast.

4. *Tell them you're considering other things.* Many executive jobseekers worry about telling a recruiter or employer that they have other offers already on the table or shortly coming to fruition.

In their mind, the employer may decide to withdraw the offer in favour of somebody else. In my experience, although this is sometimes threatened, it is rarely enforced and is purely a tactic to obtain a quick decision.

In actual fact, the sign of a good candidate is often multiple opportunities on the table at once. Providing this is fact, not fiction (an executive recruiter will have ways of checking), and providing it is communicated in a professional manner, it will have to be respected by the recruiter or employer even if he or she doesn't necessarily like it.

Often the employer's delay in making decisions throughout the recruitment process results in a competition against their competitors at this final stage.

5. *Be firm with decision deadlines.* Playing things with a straight bat is critical at the offer and negotiation stage. If the executive recruiter or employer wants a decision in a week but for whatever reason it will take you two, you need to be open, honest and firm from the outset.

If you tell them you'll have a decision by close of business on Friday, you must have a decision by then. If you can't make a decision by that time, then set a different deadline from the start.

Negotiating a better offer

Many executive jobseekers I've spoken to over the years believe that negotiating a better offer is bad practice and something not to be pursued. This belief is often due to their relief about finally finding a position and not wanting to risk doing anything that could potentially jeopardise the situation.

Think of it another way, though – wouldn't an employer expect the best candidate to try to negotiate better terms?

If the position being offered requires negotiation skills, then surely the employer would expect the chosen candidate to try to negotiate a better deal. Furthermore, an employer will often keep some powder dry. They often retain a little bit of spare capacity to improve the starting salary or to better the terms, if asked, to help seal the deal.

The last thing employers want to do is to go back to square one. If it costs them a little bit more to tip their chosen candidate over the line, this is often a small price to pay compared with the cost of running the recruitment process all over again.

After all of your hard work to get to the offer stage, there is nothing wrong with trying to negotiate a better deal for yourself, provided that you follow five golden rules:

1. *Know whom you're talking to.* Negotiating with a professional recruiter who stands between you and an employer is far easier than negotiating directly with the employer. Although it's always emotional for the recruiter when money is on the line (in the form of his or her fee), it's even more emotional when you talk to the employer directly.

Be careful not to upset or offend, and always begin any negotiation from the standpoint of how interested and enthusiastic you are about the opportunity.

2. *Know your priority.* Trying to negotiate a better salary, improved bonus and more holiday entitlement can get complicated. You shouldn't and can't negotiate on everything. Decide what your priority is, and negotiate on this point and this point alone. Depending on the complexity of your contract, there may be a couple of points you need to negotiate on, but please don't make the mistake of trying to negotiate on everything.

3. *Have a reason.* If you're looking to negotiate a better starting salary, have a good reason for it. The fact that you need more money to pay your mortgage or put your children through school is not a valid reason; although it may be important to you, it's totally irrelevant to the employer. A better reason would be an analysis of market rates at your level and in your industry sector or another

offer you've received. Always keep things factual, and never make a negotiation personal.

4. *Draw a line in the sand.* Explain to the executive recruiter or employer that if he or she honours your negotiation point, you will accept the position.

For example, if you've been offered a salary of £150,000 and say you will accept the position if offered £165,000, you must be prepared to accept at this level. If the employer revises the offer to £165,000, it's not then time to try to shoot for £175,000. Know what you want, and be happy when you get it – never be greedy.

5. *Two-way street.* Remember that negotiation can work both ways. If you open up dialogue with an employer over a better starting salary, the compromise could be (their negotiating point) reduced bonus entitlement or something similar. Be prepared for a counter negotiation, and try to anticipate it in advance.

Beware of leverage

As explained already, both the executive recruiter and the employer will want you to accept the position in a very short period. In my experience, there are two common methods to add leverage in pressuring you to make a quick decision. Don't be fooled by either of the following:

1. *Offer expiry.* It will take far longer to run a new recruitment process than to wait a few days for your decision, so take your time.

2. *There is a backup candidate.* If this candidate were as good as you are, they'd be talking to her right now, not to you. The fact that you've received the offer means they want you. They'd much prefer to hire you over a backup candidate (if one really does exist), providing you handle the negotiation process professionally and follow the rules above.

If you decide to negotiate at the offer stage, remember that the main purpose of any negotiation is to achieve better terms and to maximise your decision-making time to compare and contrast multiple offers.

At the start of this book, I introduced you to Clive. Towards the end of his calendar time period, things started to get complicated. He received one offer requiring an almost immediate decision, but he had a number of interesting opportunities in the pipeline that he was keen to explore.

To set the scene, he'd been offered a senior executive position with an organisation he was keen to join, but the money wasn't quite in line with his expectation.

Clive explained to me that he wanted more money because he'd earned more in the past – not the strongest reason to begin any negotiation. I helped him push back to the employer in a three-stage process:

1. Using other opportunities for which he was currently in the running, in addition to market information on positions in his sector and at his level, Clive had a valid reason to start the negotiation. Unfortunately, the employer stood firm and refused to increase the starting salary.

2. Next, Clive suggested that something be written into his contract to increase his salary to his required level based on hitting clearly defined targets. This was rejected, too.

3. As Clive was available immediately, the final negotiation strategy was to suggest taking the position on an interim basis for six months. From Clive's point of view, this would keep him in the game for the other opportunities he was still considering, buying him more time before he had to commit to a permanent position again.

The employer now came back quickly and increased the starting salary some way towards Clive's number – a good result for a few hours of work.

Clive negotiated calmly and professionally and had valid

reasons for wanting to better his position. The employer may not have liked it but respected Clive's position and likely sensed he could walk away, leaving the company back at square one – and thus they reconsidered and offered just enough to get him over the line. Although he didn't get quite to where he'd hoped to be, he got much closer!

FINAL THOUGHTS

The purpose of this book has been to challenge your beliefs, thoughts and actions in the executive job market. At the senior level, where opportunities are scarce and competition is fierce, it can be tempting to follow the herd in the hope that doing so will result in success.

You now know there is no such thing as safety in numbers and that to find the executive position you deserve, you have to be prepared to stand out.

You have a clear understanding of how the executive job market really works and the tools and techniques required to maintain your emotional well-being through the inevitable ups and downs of any executive job search.

Solid foundations coupled with a focused and proactive plan of attack give you a distinct advantage over your competition.

Running your own recruitment process with proven strategies and techniques that work in the real world completes the framework, serving you well both now and for the rest of your career.

You now have the knowledge, but the real test is yet to come – it's up to you and you alone to turn this into action.

Remember, you have total control over your future and the power to find and secure the executive position you deserve, not just the one you think you should be grateful to accept.

This is Career Codex, and I wish you every success for the future!

Having come to the end of this book please take a moment to review it. As I've highlighted, feedback is hugely important for self-improvement and I'd love to hear your thoughts and to find out what you found most useful. It only takes a few minutes of your time and I'm extremely grateful for every review I receive.

For additional support, training and coaching, please visit: https://careercodex.com

As we've been on a journey together, I'd be very happy to connect with you on LinkedIn at: https://www.linkedin.com/in/simongrayaca

To contact me directly, please email: simon.gray@careercodex.com

ABOUT THE AUTHOR

Simon Gray is an experienced recruiter, chartered accountant and entrepreneur. As a consultant and then founding director of his own recruitment business, he has extensive experience on the frontline, acting for both jobseeker and employer. After many years in the recruitment industry, he realised that the best way to help jobseekers at any level, was not to find them a position himself, but to empower them to find the right opportunity for themselves.

This led to the publication of his first book *Super Secrets of the Successful Jobseeker* and the formation of Career Codex (https://careercodex.com) a careers and employability training company.

Simon is an experienced speaker and commentator; he has appeared on *BBC National News at Ten* and has been quoted in *The Guardian, Financial Times* and *The Wall Street Journal.*

He is a past president of the Nottingham, Derby and Lincoln Society of Chartered Accountants and a freeman of the City of London (Merchant Taylors' Company).

In his leisure time Simon is a keen martial artist and while living and working in Japan, he completed the world-famous Yoshinkan Aikido Senshusei course with the Tokyo Riot Police.

To connect with Simon on LinkedIn, please visit:
https://www.linkedin.com/in/simongrayaca

For more information on Career Codex please visit:
https://careercodex.com

Printed in Great Britain
by Amazon